FLORENCE NIGHTINGALE AT FIRST HAND

Florence Nightingale at First Hand

Lynn McDonald

continuum

Continuum UK, The Tower Building, 11 York Road, London SE1 7NX
Continuum US, 80 Maiden Lane, Suite 704, New York, NY 10038

www.continuumbooks.com

First published 2010

British Library Cataloguing-in-Publication Data
A catalogue record for this book is available from the British Library.

ISBN 978 0826 44181 2 (HB)
978 1441 13255 0 (PB)

Typeset by Pindar NZ, Auckland, New Zealand
Printed and bound by MPG Books Ltd, Cornwall, Great Britain

Contents

List of Figures   vii

List of Illustrations   ix

Preface   xi

Dramatis Personae   xvii

A Quick Sketch of Florence Nightingale's Life   1

1 The Making of Florence Nightingale   5

   Faith and Church   8

   Domestic Arrangements, Friends, the Arts   11

   Illness and Working Style   16

   Companion Animals and Love of Nature   20

   Last Days, Will and Death   22

2 The Social Reformer   27

   Science, Law and Probability   27

   Social Class, Government and Politics   31

   Women and Family   47

   Suggestions for Thought   51

3 War   67

   The Crimean War   67

Nightingale's 'Confidential Report'   79

War Office Reform   89

The Geneva Convention, the Franco-Prussian War
and Militarism   91

Militarism and the Causes of War   94

4 Health Care, Nursing and Midwifery   99

Nightingale's Approach to Health and Healing   99

The Nightingale System of Nursing   104

The Influence of Nightingale Nursing Worldwide   113

The Evolution of Nursing Practice   125

Midwifery Training and Maternity Care   129

District Nursing   136

5 Workhouse Infirmaries and Hospitals   141

Workhouse Infirmary Reform   141

Safer Hospitals   151

6 India and Empire   159

Imperialism, Racism and Independence   163

Famine   166

Indian Women   168

7 Nightingale's Legacy   175

Endnotes   181

Recommended Sources on Florence Nightingale   189

Index   193

List of Figures

2.1   Letter to a Swedish friend from Rome   38

2.2   Letter to her family from Rome   42

2.3   The English family novel   60

2.4   The original ending of 'Cassandra'   62

3.1   Letter on failure to learn from the Crimean War   77

3.2   'Notes on the Sufferings and Privations of
       the Army'   80

3.3   'Neglect of the Orders of May'   81

3.4   The Scutari disaster   86

4.1   Advice on nursing in Belfast   115

4.2   Advice on nursing in Vienna   119

4.3   Letter on district nursing   137

5.1   Letter on workhouse nursing   143

5.2   The ABCs of workhouse reform   145

5.3   Appeal to a Conservative Cabinet Minister   148

6.1   Plea to Queen Victoria on India   164

6.2   Letter on Indian women to Lady Dufferin   170

List of Illustrations

1   Gravestone for Nightingale family, St Margaret's
Church, East Wellow   24

2   Stained glass window of Florence Nightingale at
Chautauqua, NY   25

3   Title page, *Notes on the Health of the British
Army*   66

4   Florence Nightingale statue at Waterloo Place   68

5   The 'magnificent' Barrack Hospital, Scutari   90

6   Nightingale letter on antiseptic and aseptic
practice   105

7   Nightingale statue at the Glasgow Royal
Infirmary   140

8   Nightingale paper to the East India Association
meeting   167

Preface

Why another book on Florence Nightingale,[1] even for the occasion of the centenary of her death? (Nightingale died, at age 90, 13 August 1910.) There have been books about her ever since she returned as a heroine from the Crimean War in 1856. Many celebrate her work as the major founder of the modern profession of nursing (her school opened in 1860).

Florence Nightingale at First Hand, however, differs sharply both from the large number of adulatory books portraying a self-sacrificing and brave woman (both of which are true) and from the later cynical treatments (which purport to tell the 'truth' by debunking the 'myths' about the supposed heroine). *Florence Nightingale at First Hand* reports what Nightingale said and did, based on her writing, of which a massive amount has survived, although inconveniently distributed around the world. Few of the numerous books, articles and chapters on her from any country at any time give more than cursory coverage to what she actually wrote – a pity because she was a fine writer, who told it like it is, with relentless concern for accuracy, often adding intriguing literary allusions and much humour.

The exaggerated praises of the adulatory books, many of them intended to inspire children, scarcely need refutation. They are long out of date and were probably never taken seriously. But the condescending and often derogatory second-hand books need to be answered. They have a significant and growing following. Two BBC films (2001 and 2008) using these books as sources have taken their hostile messages to large audiences. Press stories based on the television films are yet a further step away from first-hand sources. They have been more derogatory still. The widely read *Sunday Times*, in covering the second BBC film, went so far as to call Nightingale the 'liability with a lamp'.[2] Nor did any nurses or nursing organizations object, for nurses themselves don't know Nightingale at first hand and did not realize that the accusations were groundless.

Part of the problem of writing about Nightingale is that there is so much material, not only those all-too-numerous secondary sources on her, but her own letters (more than 10,000) and reports, full books, articles, briefs, letters to the editor, chapters and pamphlets in more than 200 archives worldwide. I am the person who reads it all, as editor of the *Collected Works of Florence Nightingale*, of which the first 13 of the total 16 volumes have been published (to 2010).

The purpose of this book is to present Nightingale first hand as an author, systems thinker and pioneer public health reformer. The first chapter relates her family background and education, along with the core principles that guided her working life: her faith, politics, understanding of social science and statistics, and working style. Chapters on her major areas of work follow, on social reform, women, war, public health, nursing, midwifery, workhouses, hospitals and India. A final chapter comments on her lasting legacy.

What happened to the saintly 'lady with the lamp'? Nightingale in fact was always controversial. There were hostile, often sexist, comments on her even in her lifetime. Lytton Strachey's whimsical 1918 putdown, in his *Eminent Victorians*, started the serious downward course. But the real toppling from the pedestal occurred with the 1982 publication of a book by an Australian historian, F. B. Smith, which gave the impression of being based on extensive research using primary sources.[3] (Lytton Strachey's chapter, by comparison, cited no primary sources and did not purport to be a scholarly assessment.) But Smith's *Florence Nightingale: Reputation and Power* gave copious endnotes citing original sources, and he did actually use eight archives with Nightingale manuscripts, two of them major ones. Clearly he missed most of the important archives, even the two largest for family letters, which did not stop him from making withering remarks about her family relations. More to the point, his extreme accusations turn out not to be based on the sources listed in his endnotes, when one takes the trouble to look them up. F. B. Smith's book was extolled as an exposé: finally the truth was told about this imposter. To be fair, neither reviewers nor later authors citing an academic book are expected to check the author's sources. But it is odd that so many failed to wonder how such bizarre statements could be true. Smith's error-prone charges include (without a shred of evidence) blatant dishonesty, exaggeration and cheating, appropriating junior nurses' and other colleagues' material, even the intention, if not carried out, of embezzling from the Nightingale Fund to publish personal material! (In this last case, the reference is to Nightingale's *Suggestions for Thought*, which she had privately printed and paid for herself.) Reviewers and authors not only uncritically repeated Smith's most far-fetched conclusions, but sometimes even embellished them. Some of the most enthusiastic Smith followers were junior academic nurses who subsequently became prominent in their field. It seems that they never rethought their youthful endorsement of this unreliable work.

Other social trends have contributed to detract from first-hand treatment of Nightingale's work. Nursing history has always been an extremely rare and poorly funded specialty. Nursing faculties in recent decades have typically stopped giving even a cursory introduction to their most illustrious founder, if they ever did. We look to the future, not to the past, nursing leaders say.

Heroines became unfashionable in the late twentieth century, Nightingale not the least of them. She was particularly vulnerable as a Victorian, single, celibate woman of a privileged background. That she was a radical thinker, a political liberal, with republican leanings no less, and a devout Christian believer with wide ecumenical and even inter-faith sympathies, seems scarcely to have been noticed. That she, as a nurse, led a team of male medical doctors and political figures to work for radical reforms in public health is similarly unknown. Those aspects of Nightingale's person and work escaped the attention both of the awed and inspired early writers, and the hostile and negative authors of later years.

Altogether a whole generation of readers, including nurses, doctors and public health experts, have heard little of Nightingale's ground-breaking achievements, but have been increasingly exposed to cynical aspersions or wild speculations. Is it not time now to look at what she in fact wrote and did?

On her return from the Crimean War Nightingale was determined that such high death rates as occurred in the British Army's hospitals should never recur. She set to work on a 900-page analysis of what went wrong, and succeeded, with her collaborators, in getting a royal commission to investigate and report publicly. She did much of the behind-the-scenes work for it. The BBC film of 2008 then blames *her* for the high death rates, because they happened at 'her' hospital (the one to which the British Army sent her). Her report, which evidently was not read, cites clearly who did what and when, to address the problems, and who failed to act. Moreover, her 900-page report cites a completely different hospital, at Koulali, as the one with the highest death rate, but these critics seem not to have read it.

That BBC film also lacks ordinary common sense: since when have nurses (or doctors) been responsible for the faulty sewers and overflowing toilets of the hospitals to which they are sent? Why did the army not send out their engineers when the defects were first reported? They, after all, had both the doctors and engineers who knew what was needed; Nightingale had access to neither. She developed and sustained a superb network of experts to consult later, but that was *after* the Crimean War, indeed on the basis of her analysis of the mistakes of that war.

Old-fashioned sexism continues to mar the portrayal of Nightingale. She was denounced in her lifetime for her pioneering analysis of maternal mortality post-childbirth, which was critical of doctors. An anonymous note in a leading medical journal at the time rejected her conclusions as the failure of her 'kind womanly heart'.

The BBC film from 2008 is a more recent example of sexism, where Nightingale is said to have had a 'spiritual and emotional breakdown' when she supposedly realized the errors of her work. She was then supposedly rescued by her father, who persuaded her to reform civilian nursing to expiate her failures. Her father in fact thwarted her desire to work for years, and took little interest when she finally did become a nurse. He neither shared her ardent faith nor believed in her reform mission. Further, as material in this book will show, Nightingale was long and early determined to tackle nursing in regular hospitals, and would have started in the 1840s if her family had allowed her to (it was only on the strength of her Crimean War fame that she got the chance later). Nightingale in fact claimed guidance from God for her great mission, not her earthly father. But perhaps it is too much to expect the Faith Department of the BBC, the unit that produced this film, to have a director or writer who might entertain that possibility.

If you want to read another book of sarcastic, sexist inferences, or one which shoots the messenger for bringing the bad news, read no further: this book is not for you. If you want to discover Nightingale as she was to her collaborators, some of the greatest minds and boldest reformers of her age, and how she attracted them to work with her to realize her vision, this is. If you want to discover a woman who gave much of her life to making nursing a respectable and well-paying profession for women (when none other was open to them), who reflected intelligently on the political and social movements of the day, who made friends of her colleagues and was 'mother-chief' to her own nurses, read on. Whether or not she talked to God about her mission, as she claimed, is not for me to say. It is arguably a better explanation for her life's work than guidance from her rich, well-intentioned, but lackadaisical papa.

Dramatis Personae

Frances (Smith) Nightingale (1788–1880), mother
William Edward Nightingale (1794–1874), father
Parthenope Nightingale, Lady Verney (1819–90), sister
(Sir) Harry Verney (1801–94), brother-in-law, Liberal MP
Mary Shore Smith (1798–1889), 'Aunt Mai', confidante
Henry Bonham Carter (1827–1921), cousin, secretary of the
    Nightingale Fund

Selina Bracebridge (1800–74), family friend
Lady Dufferin (1844–1936), Vicereine of India
(Dr) William Farr (1807–83), physician, statistician
Gathorne Hardy (1814–1906), President, Poor Law Board
Sidney Herbert (1810–61), Secretary of State at War, friend
Agnes E. Jones (1832–68), matron, Liverpool Workhouse Infirmary
Benjamin Jowett (1817–93), Master of Balliol College
(Sir) John McNeill (1795–1883), doctor, friend
John Stuart Mill (1806–73), political philosopher, Liberal MP
Harriet Martineau (1802–76), author, friend
Lord Panmure (1801–74), Secretary of State for War
Angelique Lucille Pringle (1846–1920), Matron, Edinburgh
William Rathbone (1819–1902), philanthropist, Liberal MP
(Dr) John Sutherland (1808–91), physician, sanitarian
C. P. Villiers (1802–98), president of the Poor Law Board
Sarah E. Wardroper (c.1813–92), Matron, St Thomas' Hospital

A Quick Sketch of Florence Nightingale's Life

Florence Nightingale was born in 1820 in Florence, Italy, the second daughter of wealthy English parents taking an extended European wedding trip. She was raised in England at country homes in Derbyshire and Hampshire. She was educated largely by her father, William Edward Nightingale, who had studied classics at Trinity College, Cambridge. At age 16, Nightingale experienced a 'call to service', but her family would not permit her to act on it by becoming a nurse, which was then a lower-class occupation and a thoroughly unthinkable pursuit for a 'lady'. Lengthy trips to Rome (1847–48) and Egypt and Europe (1849–50) were allowed. She had earlier (1837–39) been taken on a long trip with her family, mainly to Italy and France. These European trips not only improved her language skills (she was fluent in modern French, German and Italian), but exposed her to republican politics and Italian independence (she was in Rome and France during the revolts of 1848).

Nightingale managed a brief visit to the Lutheran Deaconess Institution at Kaiserswerth-am-Rhein, near Düsseldorf, Germany, at the end of her 1849–50 travels. Its hospital, orphanage and teacher training gave women opportunities for serious work and she wanted to come back for a longer stay. Her parents finally permitted her to spend three months there in 1851, to get some practical experience, and then several weeks in 1853 with Roman Catholic nursing orders in Paris. In 1853 her father gave her an annuity to permit her to become the superintendent of a small hospital, the Establishment for Gentlewomen during Illness, Upper Harley Street, London. She left it in 1854 to lead the first team of British women nurses sent to war, after the outbreak of hostilities in the Crimea. The British Army was poorly prepared for what became known as the Crimean War, and the death rate from preventable disease was seven times that from wounds. The Barrack Hospital at Scutari, where Nightingale was stationed, was structurally unfit to be a hospital, had defective drains and had to be re-engineered by a team of visiting experts before the death rate could be brought down. It had not been intended for use as a hospital and should never have been used as one. Yet when it was inspected, by Dr John Hall, inspector general of hospitals, it was given a glowing report. Nightingale herself nearly died of 'Crimean fever', probably brucellosis, caught while there.

On her return from the war in August 1856 Nightingale set to work to ensure that the high death rates that had occurred there would never happen again. Recognized as a national heroine, she chose to use that renown to work behind the scenes for structural reforms, first in the army itself, then in the wider society. She began by lobbying to get a royal commission established to investigate the causes of the medical disaster and recommend changes. She herself briefed witnesses, analyzed data and strongly influenced the thrust of the report, despite falling ill before it was finished. At the same time she wrote a 900-page analysis of what went wrong, which she had printed for private circulation.

Nightingale had only one relatively healthy year after the war. An invalid for the most part, she saw people on a one-on-one basis, making her influence through research and writing. The illness was certainly painful and incapacitating, but Nightingale learned how to work around it, focusing her best hours on the projects that had the best prospect of saving lives.

Her ardent and consistent liberal politics informed her social reform work. Her family (and the Verney family, into which her sister married) were strong Liberals. Her brother-in-law was a Liberal MP, as were a number of cousins and family friends. Letters to Indian officials who were known Liberals often have personal messages and political gossip added. Nightingale herself gave money to the Liberal Party and even wrote campaign letters for a small number of favoured (especially progressive) candidates. At a time of considerable political flux her politics were consistent: she was a thorough 'small l' liberal in her ideas, a supporter of freedom of inquiry, expression and religious toleration. The Liberal Party seemed to her to be the best political manifestation of these principles. As with the Church of England, the Liberal Party often failed to live up to them – she desperately wanted it to be as liberal on India as it was on Ireland. She stuck with both church and party.

For most of her long working life Nightingale was confined to her room, describing herself variously as 'a prisoner to my room' or even 'a prisoner to my bed'. Some days she could not see anybody, but usually she had interviews, sometimes several and sometimes lengthy ones, with nursing leaders, medical experts, politicians and Indian officials. Many people who requested interviews with her over their concerns were turned down. Time with family and friends took second place, fitted around this 'business', 'my Father's business', as she quoted it from Jesus. People who did not get interviews, however, normally got letters in reply, sometimes with detailed advice as to what to do, and even a (modest) donation.

Nightingale's own network of colleagues and advisors was impressive, and she continued to add to it as newer and younger experts, Cabinet members and MPs came into office. She always worked collectively, seeking advice and having her own questionnaires, draft articles and reports vetted by knowledgeable people.

Nightingale continued to produce papers and reports of various kinds well into her seventies. She did not do any serious writing in her eighties, when blindness and failing mental faculties gradually stopped her. From 1902 she wrote only brief messages. She died at age 90 and was buried in the churchyard of St Margaret's, Wellow, her family's parish church. Consistent with her wishes, the family declined an offer of burial at Westminster Abbey.

1

The Making of Florence Nightingale

The Nightingale parents returned to England in 1821 to raise their Italian-born daughters. They lived in great luxury, dividing their time between two country homes, Lea Hurst, in Derbyshire, and Embley Park, in Hampshire. The Nightingale fortune came from 'Mad Uncle Peter', who had made his money from lead quarrying and mining in Derbyshire.

W. E. Nightingale supervised his two daughters' exceptional education. The curriculum included modern languages, Latin and Greek, and constitutional history as well as the more conventional grammar, composition, English literature and music. Nightingale loved the classics of her own language, frequently quoted Shakespeare and Milton, and read such contemporary novelists as Charles Dickens, Elizabeth Gaskell and Harriet Martineau. She read contemporary poets like Victor Hugo, and loved adventure stories.

Numerous relatives on both sides visited for weeks at a time. The family enjoyed outings, picnics, musical performances and amateur theatre. When Embley underwent a major renovation in 1837–39 the family took an 18-month trip to France, Italy, Germany and Switzerland. The stay in Florence included lessons in Italian, art, piano and singing. The family attended a ball at the Duke of Tuscany's. They went to the opera three times a week and Nightingale said she could have gone every night.

In Geneva the tone changed completely as Nightingale's family met Italian political refugees (most of northern Italy was then under Austrian rule and the resistance had begun). The contrast between the luxury and pleasure of Florence, which had its freedom, and the rest of the occupied country, came home to Nightingale. In Geneva she met refugees suffering poverty for their beliefs. The Italian historian Sismondi took her on long walks during which they discussed politics and economics. The family returned to England in 1839 and the two sisters were formally presented at court. Normal life resumed, but Florence Nightingale had had her first taste of political struggle and would be a partisan of independence movements thereafter.

Nightingale's interest in nursing emerged in early childhood. While still a girl she began to nurse sick relatives, servants and villagers. In 1845, by then in her mid-twenties, she sought to learn nursing at nearby Salisbury Hospital. Her mother and sister were vehemently opposed. Nursing was then an unskilled occupation, poorly paid and disreputable. The stereotype has nurses drinking too much and using coarse language, although Nightingale herself refuted the latter, though not the former. The years of lost opportunity continued to rankle in old age. As late as 1900 she recorded that she 'never had a happy moment till I went into hospital life', and then 'never had an unhappy moment'.

If the 1837–39 travels in Europe sparked Nightingale's political interests, another stay in Rome in 1847–48, and travels in Egypt and Europe in 1849–50, were formative for her intellectual development. Both were taken with family friends, Charles and Selina Bracebridge, an older, childless, couple, who later accompanied her to Scutari in the Crimean War. In Rome Nightingale not only visited art museums and churches, she did detailed sketches that developed skills she later applied to hospital design. She was especially moved by the beauty of the Sistine Chapel. Seeing it, she recounted to her sister, was like seeing heaven. This was a dramatic time for the Italian Risorgimento, or National Independence Movement. Nightingale attended a great rally in the Roman Colosseum; she cheered the hoisting of the tri-colour flag at the Capitol. Moved by the struggles of the Italian cities for liberty, she praised Pius IX for giving up the papacy's temporal powers. But he would soon become reactionary (on which more below).

The trip from Cairo up and back down the Nile exposed Nightingale to a radically different society, largely Muslim, with some Coptic Christians, a peasant society with slavery, and a sophisticated capital. Cairo was 'the most beautiful city in the world', according to Nightingale in 1850. One day she dressed like a Muslim woman to attend prayers at a mosque, to see how her 'fellow creatures worshipped'. Nightingale would never visit India, but her time in Egypt gave her experience of a large and complex agrarian society, with radically different cultures and religions.[1]

While in Egypt Nightingale read the available anthropological literature, to compare the Egyptian religion with Judaism and Christianity. She accepted the expert opinion that the ancient Egyptian religion was, for its priests, monotheistic – the multiplicity of gods was to placate the uneducated. Different gods were in effect different aspects of the one God. The Christian trinity could be seen as a parallel of several Egyptian trinities.

She wrote lengthy descriptive letters home from Egypt, which her sister later had printed for private circulation. But the private diary Nightingale kept shows that the trip was a time also of anguished religious reflection. Nightingale had done a form of retreat while in Rome in 1848. On the Nile she pondered the questions and admonitions of the 'madre', Laure de Ste Colombe, who had advised her in Rome. She was painfully aware of her unacted on 'call to service'.

There were also political insights. Nightingale came to realize why only Moses, of all the Jews captive in Egypt, could lead them to Israel. Only Moses had lived as a free man (he had been raised by a princess, on his mother's leaving him in the rushes on account of the pharaoh's decree that Jewish babies should be killed).

When Nightingale was at the Kaiserswerth Deaconess Institution in 1850 and 1851 it was run by its founder, Pastor Theodor Fliedner, and his second wife, Caroline Fliedner. The institution revived a tradition of women's service in the church dating back to biblical times. Nightingale's three months there in 1851 gave effectively no training in nursing, and the sanitary conditions were poor. But the atmosphere was serious and devout and she learned discipline and order. The nurses and patients came mainly from humble origins, which broadened her experience considerably. She had an enormously enjoyable time with people who shared her deepest beliefs and were committed to pursuing their own calls. Her meritocratic inclinations were reinforced.

FAITH AND CHURCH

Florence Nightingale was baptized (while still an infant in Florence) and largely raised in the Church of England. The family back in England attended the Church of England in Hampshire, a dissenting chapel (but not Unitarian) in Derbyshire. Although three grandparents were Unitarian, the only one she knew, her father's mother, was a staunch Church of England evangelical. Her parents were married in the Church of England, by an evangelical clergyman, at St Margaret's, Westminster, next to Westminster Abbey. They did not attend Unitarian chapels after that.

Nightingale made no secret of the experience of a literal 'calling' from God, a 'call to service' on a precise date, 5 February 1837. That this was preceded by an experience of 'conversion' in 1836 (no precise date mentioned) has escaped the notice of biographers and commentators prior to the publication of the *Collected Works*.[2] This experience appears only once in her writing, as a recollection in old age. The experience was prompted by reading a book by an American Congregational minister and educator, Jacob Abbott, *The Corner-stone, or, a Familiar Illustration of the Principles of Christian Truth*.

Nightingale remained in the Church of England for the rest of her life, although she often despaired of the paltry roles it accorded women, the minimal demands it made of its adherents in general and its social conservatism.

God, for Nightingale, was a perfect Creator who made and ran the world by *laws*, which human beings could ascertain by rigorous, preferably statistical, study. With the knowledge thus gained, people could then intervene for good, becoming God's 'co-workers'. Ongoing research is required, for human interventions – however well motivated – could have negative unintended consequences. This approach appears in all the work Nightingale did.

To guide her in the research needed to discover 'God's laws', Nightingale developed an effective methodological approach. Her sources were the Belgian statistician L. A. J. Quetelet on the conduct of research and the British philosopher John Stuart Mill on its philosophical grounding.

As a young woman Nightingale considered conversion to Roman Catholicism, but did not seriously pursue this. Indeed she became increasingly critical of Catholicism over the years, identifying as a liberal, broad church member of the Church of England, and, more significantly, simply as a (Protestant) Christian. She drew on a wide range of sources for spiritual nourishment, including Roman Catholics (from the church fathers through the medieval mystics to the French, liberal Dominicans of her own age). Protestant sources also ranged widely, from the German historical school, to Puritans, the seventeenth century 'metaphysical' poets and contemporary sermons and tracts. Wesleyan influences date from her own chapel attendance early in life, and an enduring respect for church reformer John Wesley.

Nightingale's faith is key to understanding her work. She believed that God wanted people to work to change the world, not to pray to be spared the natural consequences of bad conditions. The litany of her own church included a long list of things for which the faithful prayed, including deliverance from 'plague, pestilence and famine'. It was 'impertinence to God', Nightingale told her sister in 1853. Better to clean up the sewer system: 'You pray against "plague, pestilence and famine", when God has been saying more loudly every day this week that those who live ten feet above a pestilential river will die, and those who live forty feet will live. And you want *Him* to alter *His* plans and you won't do a thing to alter yours. You pray against "battle, murder and sudden death", when God has said every year that, if the present state of education in Great Britain continues, there *will* be 999 murders in Great Britain annually'.[3]

In 1857, or early post-Crimea, and still early in her own social reform work, Nightingale wrote her father:

> I am sorry that you will not enter the House of Commons in this world, but I am very sure that there is a House of Commons in the next, I hope one upon sounder principles. If *that* world is in advance of *this*, it must be. If not, we must go and 'prepare a place' for them. Do you believe that God's word is *not* 'pray' but 'work'? Do you believe that He stops the fever, in answer not to 'from plague, pestilence and famine, good Lord, deliver us', but to His word and thought being carried out in a drain, a pipe tile, a wash house? Do you believe that mortality, morality, health and education are the results of certain conditions which He has imposed? Then you must believe that Houses of Commons, or similar institutions, are far more certain than churches to exist in all worlds till we become like God.[4]

Nightingale's decision not to marry was a logical consequence of her call to service. At that time there were no effective means of contraception, so the very life and health of a wife was entirely subject to forces beyond her control. Wives were legally obliged to obey their husbands, whose conjugal rights were unlimited. Nightingale, however, was apparently heterosexual and seems to have regretted that her life would be without a husband and physical love. She did not regret not having children, but rather took on motherly roles both with young soldiers and nurses.

Nightingale's most suitable suitor was Richard Monckton Milnes, poet, MP and philanthropist, later Lord Houghton. She refused him in 1849 but the two remained on good terms; he served for years on the Nightingale Trust, as did his son on his death. Nightingale biographer Cecil Woodham-Smith believed that Benjamin Jowett proposed to her, but this is doubted by Jowett's biographer. The evidence, albeit second-hand, comes from a reputable source; a former student of Jowett's, Cornelia Sorabji, in her memoirs, *India Calling: The Memories of Cornelia Sorabji*.[5] There Sorabji relates his confiding this to her late in life. At age 30 Nightingale recorded the recognition that *all* her suitors had married (although it seems two or more later turned up). With the benefit of hindsight she later said that not marrying was one decision she never regretted.

She described the problem of marriage as the narrowness of *family* life, explaining that a woman, even more than a man, must remain single if she has 'a work of God to do in the world'. God could not make a woman His help-*meet*, because her *'family life* is expressly fashioned to waste her time for any great object of God's'. As she put it in *Suggestions for Thought*: "'For joy that a *man* is born into the world", Christ says. And that *is* a subject of joy. But a woman must be born into the *family*. If she were born into the *world*, it would be joy too. But what joy is there in her being born into the smallest of all possible spheres, which will exercise perhaps no single one of her faculties?'[6]

On her sister's marriage to Sir Harry Verney, a widower and MP, Nightingale considered that she had done well, on balance, but her words fall short of a ringing endorsement of the married state. Sir Harry was 'active, has a will of his own and four children, ready-made, which is an advantage'.[7]

DOMESTIC ARRANGEMENTS, FRIENDS, THE ARTS

Nightingale was a gentlewoman: that is, she never worked for pay, cooked her own meals, shopped, cleaned or did her own laundry; from girlhood she had her own maid. Her death certificate described her occupation as 'of Independent Means'. Her family socialized with the great landowners and nobility of her country, and when they travelled (with multiple servants) they were received by ambassadors and dukes. Nightingale dressed in accordance with the norms of her class, although in later years, as an invalid, this meant a plain black silk dress and fine lace to cover her hair. The income her father gave her when she was allowed to work was adequate for a comfortable lifestyle and the management of her 'business', which required a fair outlay for books, documents, messengers, transportation and printing, and for modest donations to her various causes. A long-term lease her father arranged in 1866 permitted her to settle down in one place. Yet she, like Jesus, never owned any property and always lived, after she left home, in rented, borrowed or leased accommodation. Unlike Jesus, she inherited money and invested it, so that she left £36,000 in her will.

While Nightingale lived comfortably on South Street, near Hyde Park, in London, the house was not large and faced a pub, the site of 'disgraceful scenes' where 'drunken women' rolled 'in the mud'.[8] By sticking her head out the window she could see a slice of Hyde Park (and observe political demonstrations and processions). Nightingale's landlord was the immensely wealthy Duke of Westminster, later a member of the Nightingale Trust and supporter of nursing reform. She declined his 'munificent offer' of a low rent.[9] She would have been pleased, however, if he had not renewed the lease for the scruffy pub across the street.

It seems there were times when Nightingale was short of money, for she had to borrow from her lawyer. In 1900 she had to let a nurse go, although it caused her pain to part with her, but 'I am compelled to retrench'.

Nightingale's only form of asceticism was her utter devotion to work, keeping it up despite illness and fatigue. Otherwise she enjoyed the creature comforts of her class and age, and did not begrudge them to others. To ailing friends and colleagues she sent tempting food and drink (to a dying nun she sent fresh eggs, jelly, beef juice, port and champagne). She maintained a staff of five or six. Her rooms were well furnished and with, for her era, unusually little clutter. Consistent with her fanaticism for ventilation, her windows were curtainless. Visitors and biographers commented on the overall light and pleasant effect.

The food she ate and provided her guests was similarly of good quality, but simple. Surviving notes include recipes in her own hand. Nightingale was fastidious about housekeeping. A letter to engage someone for a thorough cleaning notes: 'The floor, I am sorry to say, *always* has a close, musty smell . . . Whether it is our fault I cannot say. Above all, I want freshness'. She noticed and loved flowers. A steady stream of greenery flowed into her London home from Embley, much of which she relayed to hospitals. Her friend William Rathbone regularly sent her flowering plants. She thought that flowers had a 'civilizing' effect and urged their use in hospitals, workhouse infirmaries and nursing residences. When she sent rhododendrons to be planted at a Belfast workhouse infirmary, she recommended 'flowers, plants, a canary or a singing bird in a cage, a tame cat which will not hurt the canary'.

Nightingale was a believer in moderation in drink. Soldiers, she thought, should drink less and nuns more. She sent bottles of wine to convents, and for an ailing nun 'an enormously expensive very old brandy'. How much she and her guests drank is not clear, but there are routine expenditures for beer and brandy recorded in her account books. She supported cafes for soldiers, to give them options for socializing without recourse to alcohol.

The question is frequently asked, how one can like such a paragon of virtue or such a dedicated maniac for work, or the assertion is simply made that 'you cannot really *like* her, however much you might admire her'. True, Nightingale was a formidable genius, heroine, intellectual, workaholic perfectionist; she was utterly faithful in her service and a brilliant writer, too. She also had more normal human qualities: a temper, a wicked sense of humour and considerable style. She had few friends in the normal sense – rather her friends were her collaborators in some cause or other. These were real friends, however, who shared confidences and jokes as well as books and documents. To Sidney Herbert she once sent some material Dr Sutherland had 'stolen . . . a practice I learnt from the army and taught him'.

Greetings, condolences, prayers and gifts went back and forth. Nightingale was glad of the Turkish towels; she sent pheasant and partridge. Her team, at least the inner circle who were welcomed to her home, were well fed while they were at work. Other people were kept at a distance, with careful, often affectionate, correspondence – gifts, too – but not everyone got inside the door. Former pupils who became matrons went back to her year after year for advice and sympathy. She gave them moral support and practical help in their crises, sent food parcels, flowers and books to cheer them up.

Nightingale supported her friends' causes as they did hers. There are numerous letters with money or a cheque, usually small amounts, with a supportive letter and the wish she could send more. For example, Nightingale sent a guinea to Mrs Fellowes (wishing it were ten times more) toward a harmonium for a ward at St Thomas' Hospital. For the Gordon Boys' Home she sent £5 for books and magazines. She sent money to hospital matrons for use at their discretion for needy patients – with instructions not to consult any committee, but 'to supply any wants of patients you thought pressing, any little amusements'. She gave £30 for convalescent cottages in memory of Sidney Herbert, and also worked on the plans for the (model) buildings. Serious disasters, like famine in India and the siege of Paris in the Franco-Prussian War, got larger donations, indeed concerted fundraising efforts.

Nightingale was fiercely loyal to old friends and villagers around Lea Hurst. To a woman she had taught in a class of adult mill girls in the 1840s she sent food and clothing in her old age, obtained medical care for her and mourned her death in 1888. She corresponded with former tenants and employees, and had them visit on later occasional stays at Lea Hurst. In a letter to her brother-in-law, on his asking her to invite her friends to Claydon while she was staying there, she said: 'I could not bring all Lea and Holloway here'. Reading letters *to* her, one gets the impression of enormous kindness and care, extended to a vast number of people – nurses, nursing students, matrons, former employees, villagers, colleagues and 'waifs and strays'.

Nightingale's privileged upbringing included a rich introduction to the arts. As a girl she was given music and art lessons. She attended concerts and was taken to the leading art museums of the Western world. She was 'music mad' for opera, especially Mozart. To a friend she recounted hearing the Swedish soprano Jenny Lind in London in 1847, 'but it really requires a new language to define her . . . she must be felt, not talked about'.[10] (The same Jenny Lind later gave a concert which raised £2,000 for the Nightingale Fund.)

In her curriculum vitae for Kaiserswerth, Nightingale recognized that she had 'the strongest taste for music', but that God, in mercy, took away her voice by constant sore throats. Otherwise, if she could have sung, she would have 'wished for no other satisfaction. Music excited my imagination and my passionate nature so much'. In *Notes on Nursing* she observed that the music of wind instruments, including the human voice, had a soothing effect on invalids, but the piano did not. Keen as she had been on the piano, when she was ill she found listening to it, even Mendelssohn, nerve-wracking.

Nightingale loved architecture and had the opportunity to visit great churches, palaces, abbeys, temples and mosques. Seeing Michelangelo's painting in the Sistine Chapel was a high point in her young life. The subject of the Sistine fresco, *The Last Judgment*, is a gloomy one. It would never have been Michelangelo's choice (this was commissioned art) and Nightingale herself did not believe in hellfire or damnation. Yet she bought engravings of the ceiling in Rome and kept them in her rooms for the rest of her life.

Architecture for Nightingale was 'the fittest homage' of people to God, for words were 'too precise and limited', while 'painting must be an imitation', sculpture 'too intellectual and music too sensual'.[11] Thinking of the dome of St Peter's in Rome, architecture was 'perhaps the worthiest tribute (because the farthest from actual imitation, which must fall, oh so far short of even our ideal) from man to God'.[12]

It was possible for an invalid to keep up with literature without travelling, and this Nightingale did. Although her reading was overwhelmingly of business – official reports and statistics – she enjoyed fiction and poetry. She gave novels as well as medical and religious books to nurses. Her tastes ranged from the classics (often in the original language) to earnest religious novels, low-brow, action-packed adventure stories and the tracts of the Society for Promoting Christian Knowledge. In her great old age Nightingale found enjoyment in the poetry she had learned as a child. She recited Shakespeare, Milton and Shelley, and sang French and Italian songs.

ILLNESS AND WORKING STYLE

Neither Nightingale nor her contemporaries ever knew the name or the medical details of the disease, brucellosis, that, to the best of our knowledge today, nearly killed her in the Crimean War, and which returned in its chronic phase a year after she returned to England.[13] Brucellosis is commonly transmitted from cows, sheep and goats, all of which were present at Scutari.

The symptoms include headache, poor appetite, backache, weakness and depression, from all of which Nightingale suffered. Patients may also enjoy significant periods of remission, which she did also. The disease was identified only in 1887, by Sir David Bruce, an Australian-born microbiologist at the Royal Army Medical Corps. There was then no cure for it and only some relief from the pain, for example with opium. There is still no effective vaccine for brucellosis, which is now a rare disease in industrialized countries (veterinarians and farmers are the most vulnerable). Antibiotics are effective in treatment, but these of course came into use only in the 1950s. To cope with the disease Nightingale harboured her physical resources, working as much as she could every day. She used whatever hours of the day she could for writing. She saw few people, preferably only one a day (when more than one she spaced them). Even her parents came separately because of the strain.

After her brief period of activity on return from the Crimean War, there is much of a sameness about Nightingale's life. She was effectively an invalid for life after 1857, at age 37. She stayed in her rooms, receiving visitors, mainly her inner circle of collaborators. Blue books and other official documents were sent to her. She carried on a massive correspondence with experts of all kinds. She kept a substantial library of books, official documents and journals. She did not travel farther than the country homes of her parents, sister and a few friends (within a few hours of London by train). When her (male) colleagues went on their month's fishing or grouse shooting, Nightingale stayed back in London and worked. There would be no more opera or art museums.

Nightingale's normal practice on country visits was to take her work with her. She advised government offices and other correspondents where to send the next batch of documents. She bade her co-workers meet with her at her temporary headquarters, and they, of course, complied.

Nightingale did not leave London when the House of Commons was in session so that she could respond to developments. She once explained to her MP brother-in-law that she could not go to Embley because the new minister was expected to take a Poor Law Bill to Cabinet in November. She regretted having to leave London early in 1875, which she did only to look after her widowed mother, but she missed an opportunity in delicate negotiations with the India Office on irrigation. Since she did not take part in election campaigns, Nightingale could take a break when an election was called. A letter to her brother-in-law in 1865 remarks 'now my election holidays are over'.

As a result of her ill health, Nightingale's considerable work on the reform of the War Office, her bringing trained nursing into Britain and abroad, and all her other causes from roughly 1860 on, was all carried out from her sickroom. Her unsuccessful work opposing the Contagious Diseases Acts was similarly conducted largely by correspondence. So was her pioneering work in the establishment of district nursing in

Liverpool, a project for which philanthropist William Rathbone first approached her by letter. The establishment of trained nursing in the Liverpool Workhouse Infirmary, again at Rathbone's initiative and with his financial support, was yet another sickroom activity.

The extension of trained nursing into workhouses in London had some resemblance to the early, heady days post-Crimea. There was legislation to see through parliament, questions to organize and committees to cajole. Yet except for the first royal commission, when Nightingale herself went out to brief witnesses, this was done from her sickroom. The prodigious amount of organizational work she did during the Franco-Prussian War was again done from her home, by correspondence. So also were the years of research and writing on India. She would have liked to visit India, and certainly was invited, but illness made it impossible.

A remission in her illness in the early 1880s enabled her to make a few public appearances. Nightingale made her only visit to her nursing school, and St Thomas' Hospital, on 28 January 1882, when she went through the nurses' home and visited one ward. In November 1882 Nightingale went to Victoria Station to meet the Foot Guards returning from the Egyptian campaign, for which she had helped prepare the nursing services. In December, the guest of the Queen, she attended the opening of the new Law Courts.

In addition to the main *business* Nightingale conducted, there were numerous other causes to which she contributed. At a friend's request she often obliged with an introduction to a book or a letter to the editor. For example, in 1876 she sent a letter to *The Times* on Bosnian refugees. Sometimes she started work on a worthy project but gave it up when it met with too much resistance. Schemes to promote savings, home and land ownership among the working class is one instance – she abandoned her efforts after some years when she realized she was having no effect.

Nightingale continued to work well into her seventies, for example, advising on nursing in Irish workhouse infirmaries. She produced serious work on India also to that age. She had her last visits of St Thomas' senior nurses in 1898, when she was 78.

There is a curious division between the public and private in Nightingale's thinking and practice. On the one hand she was dedicated to the *public good*, believing in a stronger role for the public sector, variously at the national, regional and local levels. Living in a democracy (at least for tax-paying men), she was well aware of the need for wide support for her projects. Neither her own mission in the Crimean War nor sanitary reform there would ever have happened without a great public outcry, prompted and fed by the mass media. Nightingale, consequently, was careful always to have a media strategy for any serious undertaking. She was astute at getting publicity for her causes. She knew how to plant questions in the House of Commons. She lined up sympathetic reviewers for her reports and organized the sending of advance copies to influential politicians as well as to key media outlets.

Yet this paragon of publicity was also intensely private, seeking press for her *causes* but not herself. Nightingale did many good deeds anonymously, avoiding use of her name except when it was beneficial to the project. When a proposal was made to name the street she lived on in her honour, she objected strenuously, saying that she would have to 'remove at once and go to quite another street'. Her satisfaction came from solving the problem or intervening correctly, in line with the laws of social science. However much she sought to serve the common good, she saw herself as a servant of God, and her accountability was, accordingly, to God and not to any public body. God was the 'commander-in-chief'. To a nursing superintendent she affirmed: 'We serve not a committee but the Lord'. This accounts for how often Nightingale took the initiative in the projects for which she worked and how seldom she let her name be used. Although often urged to take on various projects, what she worked on was overwhelmingly what she thought most needed to be done. She then sought the necessary experts and expertise to proceed.

COMPANION ANIMALS AND LOVE OF NATURE

Nightingale was always fond of animals, especially birds, and she always had pets. Her first 'patient' as a child was an injured sheep-dog, 'Captain', and she took the precaution to boil the water before dressing his wounds. At the Parthenon she rescued an owl, which she named 'Athena', but who died prophetically when she left for the Crimean War.

Nightingale owned cats throughout her life and gave them names that reflected her preoccupations. Muff stands out, for the 'muffs' (incompetents) of the War Office, and 'Mr Bismark' for the Prussian Chancellor (reserving the correct spelling for the chancellor himself). A Persian tomcat was, appropriately enough, named Darius. She also had cats named after hospitals: Tom and Barts, appropriately. She could not understand how her sister could have a cat die in a fictional work, *Avonhoe*, which Nightingale thought had the 'true literary ring', but 'how could you let little Quick die? I never could have let poor Bismark die'. Numerous letters have survived about her cats – to the Euston station master for a lost cat on a train, to finding homes for new kittens and the perils of tomcats in rural areas.

Although not a dog owner, Nightingale could appreciate the hero-ism of dogs, and invited a particularly glowing example for a visit. This was Bob, taken by Arctic explorer cousin Benjamin Leigh Smith on a search for the lost Franklin expedition. As she described it to her goddaughter Ruth Verney, Bob saved the lives of all the men in the ship – in 'the Arctic seas, where it is all snow and ice, without a blade of grass':

> They went on till the poor *Eira* [their ship] was pinched in the ice and went down in an hour and a quarter. But Uncle Ben brought his twenty-five men and his dog, a cat, a bird and a musical box safe to shore, I mean to ice. There they lived all the dark, dark, winter.
>
> You will see how Bob caught their dinners. Uncle Ben told me: he came in

like a gentleman and laid his head in my lap and then lay down at my feet. I had a plate of milk for him, but . . . he never ate out of hours and never asked for any of the dinners he got killed for the men, more than his share.[14]

Later in life there is correspondence showing Nightingale's concern about the poor quality of veterinary care, the 'brute-like ignorance of veterinary surgeons in treating brutes'. She wrote a letter to the Royal Society for the Prevention of Cruelty to Animals inquiring about legislation for the preservation of wild birds. She decried the slaughter of birds, so great that there was only one single wild bird where there used to be hundreds. Yet there is no evidence that Nightingale pursued this subject, although her MP grandfather, William Smith, had been a staunch supporter of animal welfare during his 46 years in parliament, and she had two friends who were currently involved: Lord Shaftesbury, president of an anti-vivisection society, and John Stuart Mill, a director of the RSPCA.

At home in London Nightingale fed the birds from her window. A letter records her utter delight in birds: 'There is nothing makes my heart thrill like the voice of the birds . . . the angels calling us with their songs'. Birds, indeed, prayed along with people: 'The wind is north east – the birds did not sing their morning prayers'. When the war in Egypt was over, she exclaimed what cause for joy there was 'considering what it might have been . . . Every little bird seems to sing its praise for this great mercy'.[15] An American Roman Catholic bishop described her spirituality as being 'Franciscan', after St Francis of Assisi, famous for preaching to the birds, and now the patron saint of environmentalists.

To Sir Harry Verney, in 1890, Nightingale said: 'I never see a soap bubble when I am washing my hands without thinking how good God was when He invented water and made us invent soap. He thought of us all and thought how He could make the process of cleansing beautiful, delightful to our eyes, so that every bubble should show us the most beautiful colours in the world. It is an emblem of His spirit.

When we put our own into it and handle them too roughly; immediately they break, disperse and disappear. So I try to put as little of my own as possible into things'.[16]

Further, she said, 'Some Scotch doctor says, wait for the buds and the birds and trust in God. So I scarcely ever see that lovely thing, a bird, without thinking it teaches me to trust in God'.[17]

LAST DAYS, WILL AND DEATH

In the Victorian period death was openly discussed and people took leave of each other when the time was approaching. Some of Nightingale's letters at an impending death are deeply moving. She gave a great deal of attention to her friends' and nursing colleagues' last illnesses. There are inquiries as to their condition and prayers for them – never that death was a bad thing, but regretting their loss. Letters to the dying person express appreciation for his or her life and reminisce over mutual struggles. She sent delicacies and drink to revive fading appetites. To a nurse dying of cancer she sent (with some jelly) a nosegay: 'It sometimes gives a moment's pleasure to a great sufferer to see how God was thinking of *her* when He made those beautiful flowers'.

Nightingale attended the funeral of her grandmother Shore in 1853, but few others. Housebound, she found other ways to mourn the loss of those close to her. She sent wreaths with handwritten notes and condolences to the deceased's close family or colleagues, sometimes to their servant or doctor. For her own parents she took pains on the wording of memorial cards and the monument inscriptions (the right verses to quote). She sent flowers at Easter to the graves of her parents, and then also for her sister.

In Nightingale's understanding, death was 'going home'. She often described it as entering into a new period of service or process of perfection. A letter to her cousin, William Shore Smith, on the death of his mother (Nightingale's Aunt Mai), argued that 'nothing will ever make me believe that one whose whole life was an aspiration, such as was hers, ends in a lame and impotent conclusion such as absorption, whatever that may mean'. She added that God's plan entailed 'multiplying Himself, not absorbing into Himself'.

Nightingale wanted to know who looked after a dying young nurse, Ruth Owen, in her last days, what was being done about the funeral, and could she help? A later letter offered £2 towards the gravestone. She appreciated being sent a copy of the litany used at the funeral of her friend, Anglican Sister Mary Jones. Her concern that nurses be properly buried and recognized is evident in many places in her correspondence. On Nurse Owen's death there are four letters concerning the wreath and gravestone.

Nightingale remembered the dates of the demise of key friends and collaborators, and often remarked on the anniversaries of their death in later correspondence and private notes. She also gave concerted attention to ways to remember these people, writing eulogies and obituaries and contributing to projects in their name, notably the Herbert Hospital at Woolwich, named after Sidney Herbert, and the Gordon Boys' Home, named after General Charles Gordon. She stopped the newspapers after Sidney Herbert's death, for she could not bear to read the articles on him. There is considerable correspondence on Benjamin Jowett's death as to suitable inscriptions.

One of the last visits Nightingale received from outside her family was from a Kaiserswerth deaconess, in 1904. The two reminisced about their lives of service, 'a blessed life when we can live it for others', Nightingale told her caller. The deaconess began to take her leave, seeing that Nightingale was tiring, but was stopped and commanded to pray. She knelt down (as was the custom at Kaiserswerth) and prayed with thanks for all that the Lord had done for them. Nightingale added her own 'Amen', and 'Praise the Lord', so that the deaconess concluded that she was 'a devout Wesleyan – so with my heart full of prayer and praise I came away'.[18]

Nightingale made many wills before she died, and several times left instructions regarding her death. In 1861, when she was expecting an early demise, she decided to leave her body to science, or, as she expressed it flippantly to a friend, to 'go down to posterity in a bottle of spirits'. She sorted her papers and eliminated some. In 1862 she arranged for the disposition of the printed copies of *Suggestions for Thought*.

Seriously ill again in 1864, Nightingale gave instructions that Mrs Bracebridge (or, failing her, Mrs Sutherland) should place her, for her last days, in a *general ward* at St Thomas' Hospital, but in fact she did not need to go into hospital at all. The intention, however, tells us

1. Gravestone for Nightingale family, St Margaret's Church, East Wellow. Photograph courtesy of Ronald Francis.

much about her belief in the broad availability of good care and her dislike of privileged care for those who can afford it. (St Thomas' was a fee-paying hospital, not a workhouse infirmary, but neither was it an institution for gentlewomen.) She made another will in 1887.

A will Nightingale made in 1896 gave instructions that her papers be destroyed, with the telling exception of the India material. A codicil the following year left the papers to her cousin Henry Bonham Carter, secretary of the Nightingale Fund Council, which managed the Nightingale Trust. Detailed instructions divided up her various possessions among family and friends.

After 1896, when Embley was sold out of the Nightingale family, she did not leave her rooms in London; her last visit to the Verney's

2. Stained glass window of Florence Nightingale at the Chapel of the Good Shepherd, Chautauqua, NY. Photograph courtesy of the Reverend Michael D. Calabria, O.F.M.

home in Buckinghamshire, Claydon House, took place in 1895. There is very little writing by Nightingale in her last ten years. Her handwriting became increasingly unsteady; she was effectively blind in 1901. Her memory failed and she had to be briefed on the particulars of any visitors. In 1901 she was persuaded to accept the services of a secretary. In 1906 the India Office was instructed to stop sending her papers. In 1907 she was awarded the Order of Merit, the first woman to be so honoured, but it came too late for her either to decline it (her usual approach to awards) or to appreciate it. In 1908 she became the second woman to have the Freedom of the City of London conferred on her. We do not know if she would have accepted other honours if offered – likely not – but one must note that many of her male collaborators were made fellows of the Royal Society, privy councillors, knights and even peers, not to speak of their honorary doctorates.

Nightingale died in her sleep at 2 p.m. 13 August 1910, of 'old age' and 'heart failure', according to the death certificate. She was buried with her parents in the churchyard of their parish church in East Wellow. She was carried to her grave by six sergeants (four more than she had stipulated). There is no special marker, but the inscription on her side of the family square gravestone, as per her instructions, says only 'F. N. Born 12 May 1820, Died 13 August 1910'.

2

The Social Reformer

SCIENCE, LAW AND PROBABILITY

God governs by His laws, but so do we when we have discovered them. If it were otherwise we could not learn from the past for the future.[1]

Fundamental to Nightingale's philosophy and informing *all* her writing on social and public health reform is a notion of a created world run by laws, natural and social. This she described, briefly, as early as her *Letters from Egypt*, 1849–50, and developed the theme at length while writing *Suggestions for Thought*, 1852–60. It appears as well in the essays she wrote, most of them unpublished.

L. A. J. Quetelet's *Physique Sociale* (Social Physics) was a major source for Nightingale's conceptualization of applied social science. She copied out lengthy extracts from it and wrote her own comments and paraphrases. Like Isaac Newton, Quetelet had a sense of the immensity of the world to study and the modesty of the results to date. Echoing Newton he said, 'These are only a few pebbles picked up on the vast seashore of statistics'.[2] Yet Quetelet was for Nightingale no less than 'the founder of the most important science in the whole world, for upon it depends the practical application of every other art, the one science essential to all political and social administration, all education and all organization based on experience'. Without it, she held, government would otherwise be 'guesswork, or as the Germans would say, "intuition"'.[3]

More positively, laws told people (God's fellow workers) how to intervene: modify the causes of a problem and you modify human behaviour, 'free will and all'. God governs by His laws, but so do we, when we have discovered them. For Nightingale as well as Quetelet, free will was a red herring and she resented the loss of time and energy in debating it. Her/their understanding of law did not immobilize people but, on the contrary, enabled them to act. Laws were *descriptive*, so that it was better to designate their discovery as 'registering' them; they did not 'subject man's action in the plan of God's moral government'.

Any laws discovered were only *probabilistic*. Quetelet, himself an expert in probability theory, she commended for being 'always on his guard against confounding probability with truth'.

In an article she published in 1873, Nightingale held that 'everything down to the minutest particular is so governed "by laws which can be seen in their effects" . . . that not the most trifling action or feeling is left to chance'. Yet, while nothing occurred by chance, 'unintended consequences'[4] were frequent and serious. She often gave as examples the establishment of foundling hospitals for abandoned babies (which had high death rates), and handouts to beggars (which only increased pauperism). This was not to accept the political economists' approach of non-intervention; the goal was to intervene constructively and effectively.

Nightingale's philosophy of science is clearly in the positivist tradition, understood as the acquisition of knowledge through research in the real world, as opposed to intuition, introspection or reliance on authority. She opposed positivists when they took up atheism, or the 'religion of humanity', as Auguste Comte notably did. She sought to integrate a methodologically tough positivism with idealism in objectives. She disagreed with the treatment of idealism and positivism as 'opposite philosophies'. Rather the one was 'a necessary precursor and foundation of the other'. She asked, 'Are not the two one? . . . [for] positivism lays down that all things, moral as well as physical, are subject to law'. Positivism was the way to achieve the goals of idealism, 'the only way by which we can alter or improve anything'.

Positivism provided idealists with the tools to learn where and how to intervene for good. 'A perfect God cannot change His mind'. Positivism says universal law, or the mind of God, is never altered, while idealism says that '*He* would not be a perfect God who could alter His mind'.

Consistent with her views on social science, Nightingale supported the organizations that promoted it. For many years she sent papers to meetings of the British Association for the Promotion of Social Science, founded in 1857. She submitted two papers on hospital construction to its first congress in 1858, and sent papers regularly thereafter. Physician and leading statistician William Farr proposed her for membership in the London Statistical Society (later the Royal Statistical Society) in 1858; she was its first woman member.

As a British empiricist philosophically, Nightingale could be expected to have favourable views of philosophers John Locke and Francis Bacon, and negative views about the competing 'intuition-ist' school of German idealism. For her Bacon was a great inductive philosopher, 'much greater than Mill'.

With the benefit of hindsight it is possible to identify a Nightingale method (she never gave it such a name), which remains good advice today:

- Get the best information available.
- Use government reports and statistics wherever possible.
- Read and interview experts as well.
- If the available information is inadequate, collect your own.
- Draw up a questionnaire.
- Consult experts on it, practitioners who use the material.
- Test the questionnaire before sending it out.
- After writing up the results of the research, send out a draft or proofs to experts for vetting before publication.

All the while Nightingale's faith was energizing the process of research and reform. That she could conceive of health care as a system owes much to her conceptualization of God as the all-good Creator who runs the world by laws, capable of discovery by research. All her work in health care and social reform derived from her own call to serve this God. She sometimes described herself humbly as the Lord's handmaid, other times more confidently as a fellow worker.

For Nightingale the laws of natural and social science were fundamentally similar: both were the work of God and both were open to human discovery by induction from research results. She held, further, that the two sorts of law, social and physical, acted and reacted on each other. One important difference between them was that, while we cannot modify the solar system, we can modify the social system. We can predict an eclipse, and both predict and influence social events. She compared the two kinds of prediction in an 1873 article, 'A sub "note of interrogation" What will be our religion in 1999?'[5]

Nightingale's education included little natural science and she had to plead for some mathematics to be added to her instruction. Mathematics was not considered necessary for girls, and perhaps outside her classically educated father's area of expertise in any event. Her father did take her to a meeting of the British Association for the Advancement of Science at Oxford University in 1847, shortly after the discovery of the planet Neptune. The two discoverers of the planet were prominent participants at the congress. Nightingale was interested in the history of science and had a reasonable lay person's acquaintance with the scientific issues of her time. She made frequent references to scientists in her unpublished notes, especially of physicists Isaac Newton and Michael Faraday. Her disapproval of Charles Darwin, whose *Origin of Species* was published in 1859, was based not on any conventional objections to the theory of evolution, but on a disagreement as to the *facts*: 'Darwin has got no true principle because he had only one true fact and one hundred false ones'.[6]

When Nightingale was growing up it was commonly believed that the world was about 6,000 years old, using the estimate made by James Ussher from the lifespans of the patriarchs in the Old Testament.

This is apparent in two places in *Suggestions for Thought*. But in one place human existence was extended to 'thousands (we know not how many) of years'. The 6,000 years, or any short time span, does not appear in any of her later writing. Late in life she gave books to friends and schoolchildren on Darwinism, or 'Darwinianism' as she called it. Clearly her views on evolution and natural selection mellowed.

Naturally Nightingale disapproved of *social Darwinism*, the application of the 'survival of the fittest' thesis to social organization, which justified the *laissez-faire*, non-interventionist approach of the political economists. Arguing with Mill she denied that Darwinism was based on careful observation. Still, Darwinism was not the 'sin against the Holy Ghost', or the sin against hope: that sin was using past mistakes as an excuse for not doing *anything*, effectively the position of the political economy school.[7]

Nightingale's interest in natural science, and her optimism that knowledge could be applied for good, led her to appreciate the pioneering work on acid rain done by Robert Angus Smith in the 1860s. Dealing with him on Indian water issues in 1865, she sent congratulations on his first report as inspector under the Alkali Act, on what was probably the world's first legislated pollution abatement: 'I cannot forbear wishing you joy, and wishing England joy, of your first report on the condensation of gases from alkali works . . . You have clearly shown how advantageous it is to employ scientific men on scientific work like this, and in the end there is every prospect that you will be able to rid the country of a great nuisance'.[8]

SOCIAL CLASS, GOVERNMENT AND POLITICS

From early in life Nightingale was appalled by the enormous disparities in wealth between people such as her own family and the great mass of people, when the large majority owned no property and enjoyed few comforts, and nearly one-third of the population lived in absolute misery. She performed the usual acts of charity for the poor, but realized how inadequate they were. She developed more than a social conscience, to come to see 'the face of God' in the poor, sick and imprisoned. The gospel was her source: 'We should consider that the same tie really connects us to every one of our fellows as the tie which connects us with God. That to neglect or ill use the imbecile old woman, the dirty child, is the same crime of *lèse majesté* against the Almighty that blasphemy of God is'.[9]

Throughout her life she was sensitive to the humiliations to which people of lower status were frequently subjected. In drafting a letter to the chair of a committee of the Glasgow Royal Infirmary, a shoemaker, she advised her uncle, 'please write very respectfully'. She was concerned that her colleague, Robert Rawlinson, son of a private soldier and known for 'murdering the Queen's English', would be sent to eat with the servants when at Lea Hurst (at her behest he was assisting with sanitary improvements), although 'he is just as much a gentleman as you or I'.

Nightingale's sensibilities on class differences and discomfort with her own family's wealth emerged early and caused difficulties at home. A family friend recalled the young Nightingale dwelling on the 'painful' social differences that existed and 'the trap that a luxurious life laid for the affluent'. The friend had laughed at the time at a conversation between father and daughter; 'the contrast was so striking', but later took this as a sign of Nightingale's call.

Nightingale herself identified with the poor people on the family estate at Embley: 'I feel my sympathies all with ignorance and poverty; the things which interest me interest them; we are alike in expecting little from life, much from God'.[10] This identification with ordinary people remained throughout her working life. In the Crimean War she laboured to save and improve the lives of ordinary soldiers. Her promise that lives would never again be lost from such neglect was made with these young men in mind. Her work on sanitary reform was always sensitive to class issues. She realized that the poor could not avail themselves of clean air and water as the rich could, which meant that *public* measures had to be instituted. She recommended sending convalescent poor to the seaside: 'For the rich the good of change of air, nay, even its necessity, is never doubted. It is *ten times more* necessary for the poor'. Further, 'every large town' ought to have a convalescent institution for the poor by the seaside or in the country', she wrote in her introduction to William Rathbone's book, *The Organization of Nursing*.[11]

Nightingale was consistently meritocratic in her approach to nursing. 'Ladies' came with better education and general culture than women from other classes, and hence were advantaged for senior administrative posts. But she insisted on their having a thorough training, i.e., no exemptions or short cuts on account of their social status. They had to learn the most menial of tasks. 'Lady superintendent' in practise became a job title; some institutions used it, others preferred 'matron'. The Nightingale School sought out 'ladies' for training precisely because it wanted to influence nursing and needed to train potential matrons.

Nightingale is credited with opening up the profession of nursing to middle-class women, which she did, but seldom for making it the first and most amenable profession for working-class women. Nightingale even considered provision for girls who had grown up in workhouses to enter nursing – they would be too young to enter training directly, so she proposed employment in a hospital as an intermediate stage.

In Nightingale's day there were *no* educational prerequisites for admission to a training school. Those trained at her school, called 'probationers', were given free room and board and a small stipend. In fact, before Nightingale, working-class women did *not* nurse in Britain. Rather, they were hospital *cleaners*, although they were called 'nurses'. Those on night work had some duties as patient 'watchers'. Nightingale's reform was to separate cleaning jobs from patient care, reserving the title 'nurse' to the latter, and making it a decent, well-paying job, open on the basis of merit, regardless of class origins.

For the 1871 census Nightingale asked an official how she should describe her occupation, and objected to his reply of 'none, gentlewoman'. She joked that she would deserve to be fined 'for false information' if she replied 'no occupation' and thought that she should at least put 'war hospital matron, or hospital matron retired from active service through illness'.[12]

In fact throughout her life she gave her position as head of the Nightingale Fund and Training School on the census return, although it was never a paid position (she never held one) and she always lived on her own means.

In her decades of work on India the same identification with the poor masses held. Nightingale routinely castigated the British Government for policies that favoured the landlords and worsened the hard lot of the rural poor. The ryot, the Indian peasant, she repeatedly pointed out, was the most industrious person in the world, and should enjoy more of the product of that labour. She opposed the salt tax for its regressivity; the poor had to spend more of their incomes than the rich on salt, an essential item for food preservation. She pressed for land tenure reform and restrictions on high interest rates. Her letters and papers to Indian organizations show much fervour as well as pertinent analysis.

Nightingale shared the views of her class on labour unions as being tyrannical and losing workers' jobs by asking for too much. Yet she was pro-labour in many respects. In an article she published in 1869, she argued for better wages and salaries: 'It is always cheaper to pay labour its full value. Labour underpaid is more expensive'.[13] She also favoured better holidays for workers, especially women workers in high-stress occupations like the needle trades.

Pauperism, referring to people living off handouts when they *could* work, was abhorrent to Nightingale. An article she wrote in 1873 opened with a statement of how much was spent annually on Poor Law relief, with the result only 'to increase directly and indirectly the pauperism it is meant to relieve'. The solution was to remove all the sick and those incapable of work from the workhouses and provide for their care or cure. She was less specific about what to do for those remaining, but thought that few would choose not to work if jobs were available. She found it impossible to believe that, 'at least in exceptional times of distress, the state could not provide work at remunerative prices'. Here we can see the germ of J. M. Keynes's advocacy of counter-cyclical spending.[14] Nightingale hoped to do more research on the subject, collected material to that end and tried, unsuccessfully, to get her friend Dr Sutherland to edit it for publication.

While the ideas of many radical theorists softened with time, this did not happen with Nightingale. A letter late in life (1891) on the treatment of the people who rioted in Hyde Park and Trafalgar Square called it a 'horrible and degrading spectacle that we can do nothing for our vagabonds and unemployed but drive them from street to street with our fists – a far sadder spectacle than war'. In one of her last publications on health care she remarked on the scarcity of good nurses, even for royalty, 'but royalty can take care of itself and poverty can't'. Nightingale always wanted services to be levelled up; when middle-class women took to their beds for a month to recuperate from childbirth, she thought working-class and poor women should be able to do the same.

For a while Nightingale took on the subject of criminality, especially juvenile delinquency. Certainly she had been impressed with Quetelet's early criminological work in his *Social Physics*. She published several short articles and letters on the treatment of criminals, urging, among other things, that thieves be required to pay restitution.

Nightingale abhorred the dominant *laissez-faire* liberalism of her day, what might today be called right-wing conservatism. It had been shaped by the political economists Thomas Malthus and David Ricardo, precursors to Milton Friedman of the Chicago School of the late twentieth century, and inspiration to Margaret Thatcher and Ronald Reagan. 'The laws of political economy, if really discovered, are of course as immutable as the laws of nature, but at present there is scarcely any extravagance which political economy is not made to father, for example the workhouse test, which probably has made more paupers than anything else – the theory that supply and demand will always, under all circumstances, in all countries, answer to each other – which made the Orissa famine possible under our "enlightened rule".[15]

Nightingale was never a socialist, but rather a (lifelong) left-leaning, pragmatic liberal. She would leave the running of the economy largely to the private sector, in line with *laissez-faire* principles. Government, however, should be used to solve great social problems that could not be dealt with otherwise. Whether or not it should be called on, and what level of government, were matters for considered judgement. 'Above all it is governments which dispose of life. Is it not then the first, the most essential, step to have a political science, to raise it, if it is a science at all, into an *exact* science?'

Ever practical and cost-conscious, Nightingale recommended that *all* government programmes be subjected to evaluation: 'A government in modifying its laws, especially its financial laws, should collect with care documents to prove, at a future state, whether the results obtained have answered their expectation. Laws are made and repealed with such precipitation that it is most frequently impossible to study their influence.'[16]

To Francis Galton, an expert on probability theory and eugenics, she complained that government collected 'splendid' statistics, which it then did not use. This was one of the reasons she sought, in one of the last projects of her life, to have a chair or readership in 'social physics' (Quetelet's term) established at Oxford University, the chief place of education of the senior civil service. This would teach Quetelet's method to the people who most needed it, those actually administering social programmes.

Because of the important scope for government action in her system, legislators had a particularly important – even *holy* – role to play. Legislators had a 'noble mission', she explained in an essay on Quetelet, because they could alter the atmosphere in which we live. Politics was

the administration of God's world, 'in the particular time and place of
the nation', bringing down 'God's government from heaven to earth'.
How easy it would be if political leaders, 'in pleasing God, were really
pleasing the Cabinet, the War Office and the Poor Law Board'. Instead,
she pointed out, 'if we are to please our rulers, we must displease God,
for the House of Commons does not like at all what God likes! Oh dear
how I wish "the Lord" *was* "king" or at least prince of Wales'.[17]

Regrettably to Nightingale, people believed God to be quite inadequate to direct the business of a great nation: 'A nation would fall to
pieces if its business were done according to His will. And no wonder,
it certainly would, if done according to what we conceive *now* to be His
will . . . No wonder we exclude Him from our Cabinet, our House of
Commons, our politics, our political economy, and think that Sunday
is *His* day . . . the weekdays are ours – "Monday and Thursday" are
"government nights" in the House of Commons; God's evening is
another evening in the week'.[18]

For the Liberal Nightingales the Conservatives got short shrift.
Benjamin Disraeli was 'Dizzy' in correspondence with family and
friends. Later in life Nightingale told her family that the arch-
Conservative Lord Randolph Churchill was a 'real terror', joking that
she would change the hymn 'The devil and me/We can't agree', to 'Lord
Randolph and me/We can't agree'.[19]

Nightingale's role as a social reformer required her to work with
whatever political party was in power. There is no doubt as to her
Liberal preferences, especially in her later years when she worked
closely with her Liberal brother-in-law, Sir Harry Verney. Socialists
and Conservatives alike may be dismayed by Nightingale's insistence
that God 'is on the Liberal side'.[20] She told the wife of Verney's son
Edmund (who was then running to succeed him as MP), that in helping him she was 'working for eternity, to raise the ground, the Liberal
cause – that *is* the "saving" of men's minds, bodies and soul, that is
being fellow workers with God . . . God is a "Liberal", we may say that
without irreverence'.[21]

FRENCH POLITICS

French politics were of interest to the Nightingale family in general, and to Florence Nightingale in particular. En route to Egypt in 1849 her ship passed by Corsica, where 'towards dusk we could see the light off the place where the arch fiend [Napoleon] was born, near Ajaccio. But I would not go on deck to see the place, which is accursed'.[22]

Ironically, when the Nightingales stayed in Paris in 1837–38, they rented an apartment in the Place Vendôme, a fashionable area, and the site of the great monument to Napoleon. His statue tops a high column made from iron melted down from the cannons of the defeated Russians and Austrians at Austerlitz.

Nightingale's correspondence with a young Swedish woman whom she met in Venice, Selma Benedicks, is a delightful source of her youthful enthusiasms (she was still a teenager) and her early views on French society, politics and religion. This letter (Figure 2.1) also gave news of Italian developments, for her family had met other Italian exiles in Paris. The 'treacherous amnesty' that the Emperor of Austria had promised, she said, had opened the door to only a few. The Emperor could grant or refuse anyone, having promised a return to all. On her 1850 trip to Europe, when travelling through Austria, Nightingale and her friends passed by Spielberg Prison, where a captured resistance leader, Count Confalonieri, barely survived his 15 years imprisonment – a sentence commuted from death.

Figure 2.1 Letter to a Swedish friend from Rome[23]

Place Vendôme
28 November [1848]

We are living in a very nice apartment furnished à la Louis Quatorze in the Place Vendôme, one of the finest parts of Paris. We have that splendid column, made of the cannons taken at Austerlitz, with the statue of Napoleon at the top, which I need not describe to you, for I think you know Paris. But I do not like Paris; it is so noisy and the smoky clouds never lift up off it. The Tuileries and the Louvre together are a splendid mass of building, and the Bourse and the Church of la Madeleine, those models of Grecian temples, are finer than anything there is in London. But Paris seems so uninteresting after beautiful Italy, and the pictures in the Louvre are so bad in comparison, and it is so cold.

Do not you think the French very full of vanity when compared with the Italians? We know a great many people here, not many French, for some of our friends are not come into town yet, though this winter is a very bad one, but chiefly Italians and English. Several very, very agreeable old French gentlemen come in very often and amuse us very much by their politics and good stories, for the French are so clever in conversation . . .

Our poor friends Ugoni and Porro (the master of the beautiful villa on the lake of Como) are already refused permission to re-enter, but with an intimation, said to be put in by the emperor himself, in German, that if they conduct themselves well they may be admitted at some future time. Conduct themselves well!

What a base lying amnesty this is! It is said to be all the doing of Metternich and of the authorities of Milan and that the emperor wished the amnesty to be applied in its full sense and was very earnest to make another to admit everybody. He is a kind man, but under the rule of others completely . . . Metternich seems to be trying to disgust and humiliate the exiles in their return to their country as much as possible . . .

The greatest pleasure in Paris is, as you say, the Italian opera and we go there once a week, and I look forward to the day all the week before. They have a most splendid set of singers now.

France went through numerous changes of government during Nightingale's lifetime, from kingdom to empire to republic. When Louis-Philippe (an elected king, but of the old royal family) was toppled by Louis-Napoléon (who may or may not have been a nephew of Napoleon Bonaparte), she saw no advantage. She likened the coup to Brutus killing Julius Caesar for becoming too powerful – then his successor, Augustus Caesar, became a thorough dictator, made himself emperor and was even deified: 'He had not thought what was to come next, and there followed a worse than Caesar. In the same way the French knew very well that Louis-Philippe's Government was an evil, and they overturned him without more ado, but they had not thought about what was to come in his place, and a worse than Louis-Philippe is here. This is not saying that Louis-Philippe was not an evil and that they had better have left him alone – but that they had better have considered what they were about to place in his stead'.[24]

Again there are negative views of Louis-Napoléon, or Napoleon III, his title after he seized power in 1851: 'Look at France's submitting to such a yoke and what do we discuss? Not the chances or means of recovery for the wretched French from this horrible disease, but the personal character of Louis-Napoléon, as if the coup d'état were a play or a work of art. We dispute whether he is a fanatic or a rascal, whether he is a well-intentioned man using bad means or a bad man using good means'.[25]

Nightingale was in Paris in 1853 at the time of the spectacular wedding of Napoleon III with the woman who became the Empress Eugénie. The wedding launched the fashion of extravagant wedding dresses (previously brides were content with a fine, but more ordinary dress). Eugénie was 'born to be a dressmaker', quipped Nightingale, marrying the 'wickedest man in Europe' to become empress.[26] Nightingale did not join the throngs who went to watch the wedding procession to Notre Dame Cathedral.

ITALIAN POLITICS AND THE POPE

It is well to bear Nightingale's Italian connections in mind, as well as the French, when trying to make sense of her politics. Not only did she continue to identify with the city of her birth, Florence, she read and was influenced by its great authors, especially Dante. Nightingale threw Italian expressions into letters to friends and relatives. Thus a confusion is a 'scompiglio', a fight a 'baruffa' and a mix-up a 'garbuglio'. Even late in her life, in 1880, she could send a joking note to the Verneys in Italian, to arrange for a ride home from the railway station.

Nightingale was much taken by the 'city of God' concept of the Florentine monk Savonarola, who was burned at the stake in 1498. Florence under him became democratic in certain respects, puritanical in others – in the four years of the experiment 'pagan' paintings were burned. An excerpt Nightingale took from Savonarola's poetry reveals her identification with his martyrdom (her emphasis in italics): 'Above all things, love God with all your heart; *seek His honour more than the salvation of your own souls* . . . Lord, I ask you the grace not to die in my bed, but that of shedding my blood as you did for me'.[27] This expression of Nightingale's willingness, even desire, to die sacrificially gives context to her service in the Crimean War.

The Italian Risorgimento was the primordial independence movement for Nightingale. Her passion aroused by her trip as a teenager, she read the prison accounts of the captured independence fighters. Sardinians, in the newly emerging independent state of Italy, joined Britain and France in the Crimean War, giving further contact with Italians.

In Rome in 1847–48 Nightingale's views of Pius IX were enthusiastically positive. Newly elected and thought to be a progressive, in fact he soon sided with Austria and opposed the forces of liberation for Italy. This is understandable given that the Vatican would lose massive territories to the new, secular state. (It then held about one-third of the territory.) The liberal Nightingale would also be scandalized by the pope's enunciation of the dogma of the immaculate conception of Mary, in 1854, and of infallibility in 1870.

In an unpublished essay she jested: 'The pope is infallible because he says so. And we are to believe it because he is infallible who says so.

(Other popes have not said so and there will come again popes, if popes there be at all, who will not say so.).'[28]

Correspondence from her time in Rome, however, shows Nightingale's great enthusiasm for him. She and the friends with whom she was travelling were invited for a private audience with Pius IX. The time had to be rescheduled once as the pope was delayed elsewhere on a political emergency. They were kept waiting in his private quarters, which allowed them a glimpse of some personal things. Nightingale snuck a peak into his bedroom (see Figure 2.2).

Nightingale described the pope as 'sincerely religious – he confesses once a week', but under the influence of a 'mock saint', his confessor. Respect for the church had 'amazingly fallen'. While people used to 'fall on their knees when a cardinal passed, now they look the other way'. Meanwhile, the new, secular, governmental bodies were uncovering abuses.

Figure 2.2 Letter to her family from Rome[29]

---

17 January St Antonio [1848]

My dearest people

I am really ashamed of you – don't speak to me in that manner. I am surrounded here by enemies of Pius, and shall I find foes in mine own household? Is Pius to wait till all his convictions are made up before he acts? He would never act at all. What did we abuse all the former popes for? but because they would never listen to anybody, but went tramping on their own stupid, brutal, wicked course. Now we despise Pius because he listens and acts accordingly. I thought that old cry of consistency was blown up, sunk and gone to the bottom with the chew-the-cud thing it represents. Pius is no Napoleon in the talent of discrimination, I know that, but to be consistent a man must be either superhuman or subhuman. Now for what he really is, such as those most indifferent to him, represent him: his first desire is the good of his people – it is his *real* fervent *pursuit* that all acknowledge, but with one condition. What is that? You do not expect, as the English do here, that he is to turn Protestant, do you? . . .

I was going to tell you about the oratory of the santo padre [holy father]. The first time we went to be presented, and he was obliged to go out because of the row, we thought, as we were once in, we would do something before we were got out. I asked to see this oratory, which is never seen because he can come into it at any moment. It is the prettiest little cheerful place – one little chair in the middle for him – all in disorder just as he had left it: a heap of books on one chair, i.e., two well-thumbed, well-dog's-eared, old-woman's, bound-in-black fat Bibles, then two or three little books, missals, and then one little thin book, which looked like a Greek Testament. All looked and smelt as if it was constantly inhabited: two large bright windows, the altar quite plain, perfectly without artificial flowers or any ornament whatever, over it a large Guido of the Annunciation – on one wall the Virgin making up domestic linen and an angel on each side learning to sew from her, who are going to help her and are watching how she does it, a Padre Eterno in the little cupola with a gloria of angels looking up, a virgin in adoration, patriarchs and prophets about in odd corners. They are all Guido's very, very best.

The flamingo who showed us in, a cameriere in red, was in a great fright to get us out because there is a door into the pope's own room. But I took a good look first. Here he had evidently just been. Here he takes refuge from the troubles of his own conscientiousness (which have made him a grey old man at fifty-five), from the doubts, the difficulties (which must tear a sincere man like wild horses in twain), for he is scrupulous, and only Napoleons, without consciences, are 'consistent'.

Here he prays for light and here that beautiful angel of the Annunciation looks down upon him. When he remembers the answer of the humble, hopeful Mary, he feels that the day will come when all doubts shall be done away for him, too, when fears and hesitations shall vanish, and when those who have indeed said from their very hearts, 'Behold the servant of the Lord', as he, I verily believe, has done, shall *also* be able to say: 'be it unto me according to thy word', all anxieties being removed as to what

that 'word' is, and all fears as to whether we are not following our own
will, after all, instead of discerning what the will of God for us is. One
might have more admiration for the intellect of Pius, but one would not
have half the sympathy for him if he were not beset with anxieties. But
I hope that to him, too, the angel brings peace. I had such pleasure in
seeing his little oratory.

Nightingale credited the pope with making an unannounced inspection visit to San Spirito Hospital, where he had ordered improvements
in care. He found that they had not been carried out, and an attendant even admitted that they gave patients only half the prescription
ordered, as an economy. Nightingale had visited the hospital with
Elizabeth Herbert – while not allowed to nurse at a hospital, it was
acceptable for a lady to visit and be shown around. She took full
advantage of this privilege of her class and gender.

Nightingale passed on comments from a meeting with Orioli,
professor at Rome's Sapienza University, and leader of the moder-
ate party. She noted that he was giving a course on geology, 'the first
man who has dared to do it in Rome'. He 'wisely' opened his course
by quoting St Augustine, 'beginning with prudence', and continuing
'with boldness'.[30]

In Rome Nightingale and Mrs Bracebridge had that rare treat of
an afternoon at the Sistine Chapel all to themselves. She saw it many
times and sent home rapturous reports. The first of the compartments
of the roof, on the 'very limits of the supernatural', she did not understand. It had 'an appearance of exertion, of effort about the Creator in
the act of creation'.

Nightingale would follow Italian politics with interest all her life.
Her views on Count Cavour, Prime Minister of the young Italian state
in 1852, were highly favourable: 'Cavour [was] the real maker of Italy
into a kingdom of 26 million. No sooner had Austrian supremacy
withdrawn in 1859 (Cavour having invited Louis-Napoléon III in

against them), than all the petty despotic governments of Italy fell before the indignation of their own subjects. Cavour made Piedmont the model and standard of Italian political progress, the stronghold of political liberty'.[31] When Cavour died, in June 1861, her friend Sidney Herbert telegraphed Nightingale the news, adding: 'This is the life I should like to have lived; this is the death I should like to die'. She quoted these remarks later to a colleague, adding that he had had his wish – he died only seven weeks later. To her father she described Cavour's death as 'heroic – in the prime of his glory and success, working to the last'. She also pointed out that he had had bad medical care. To her brother-in-law, she said his loss was of 'the most valuable life in Europe. His was the cord which kept the stone on the mountainside. The cord is cut. There are none to succeed'.[32]

Garibaldi fared less well in Nightingale's esteem, as 'good, simple, gullible'. His insurgents had failed to fight in a disciplined way against a regular army: 'Garibaldi's volunteers did excellently in guerilla movements; they failed before a fourth-rate regular army'.[33] He played into the hands of the traitors. 'How could he?' He had the 'coeur d'or vraie tête d'écolier' [heart of gold but the head of a schoolboy].[34]

Nightingale agreed to receive Garibaldi when he made a triumphant visit to London in 1864. She insisted that the visit be strictly unannounced and incognito, but word got out and she got '300 letters' in consequence. The day before he had visited a factory making steam engines, hence the machine reference below. To prepare for meeting with him, Nightingale jotted down in French [here translated] what she would say, as 'the ant to the general'. 'Eh bien! in five years you have made Italy – the work of five centuries. You have worked a miracle. But even you, mon général, could not make a steam engine in five minutes. And Italy has to be consolidated into a strong machine, like those which you have been seeing at Bedford'.[35]

On Mazzini, in 1872, she commented: 'Whatever influence was left to him he was certain to exert in a way unfavourable to the true interests of his country. [His life was] purposeless, if purpose implies a *due relation between means and end* . . . Nothing has come out of his movements for twenty years. He made Italian success and unity impossible in 1848–49; practical bearings lost in ideal forms of perfect social organization, like a doctor angry with his patient for getting well without his medicines was Mazzini with Italy'.[36]

From her childhood, Nightingale was inspired by the great Roman classics, especially the Emperor Marcus Aurelius Antoninus. She especially liked a French translation of his *Meditations*, quoted from it and used to compare him with Garibaldi.

> Marcus Aurelius seems to me a Garibaldi in purity, with the administrative faculty (which he wants) and above all with the willingness to let the waves pass over his head, which is always the fate of the man of thought struggling to incarnate his ideal in politics. He thanks Rusticus, his tutor, for having withdrawn him 'from what is *purely* speculative'. He exhorts himself to '*heroic* truth in all his words'. He says (to himself): 'Thou, when thou dost not like to rise in the morning, tell thyself, "I wake to do the work of a man. Thou dost not love thyself if thou dost not love the calling of thy (better) nature. Even the artisan forgets to eat and sleep for his art's sake. Is the public interest less worthy of thy care?"'[37]

Nightingale then compared Marcus Aurelius's advice with the Christian admonition to destroy 'self-love', that you must 'hate' yourself. She preferred the (pagan) Roman's more self-asserting contention, that he was '*put into the world for the salvation of men*'. This was 'sublime', to Nightingale: '"Offer to *the God within* (*thee*) a *man*, a citizen, an emperor, *a soldier at his post, ready* if the trumpet call." Can anything be truer of the vocation of man, in general?'

Marcus Aurelius called philosophers 'children' who did not turn thought into action: 'Do not hope for a Plato's *Republic*; content thyself with making things advance somewhat'. It would be advice she herself acted on all her life, although she failed to convince Garibaldi to settle for such mundane improvements.

Garibaldi had spent some years in Britain in exile, and loved British political institutions. Nightingale shared with him the feeling, as she told her brother-in-law during the 1880 British general election: 'I, like Garibaldi, cannot pass the House of Commons without tears'.[38]

WOMEN AND FAMILY

Nightingale held that women have the same right to develop their abilities as men – to become perfect, in her terms. She accepted conventional gender roles somewhat less than her contemporaries. That she wanted women to become nurses rather than doctors was largely practical: women did not have the education for medicine and medical prejudice was then formidable. It would be a century before women would enter medical schools in large numbers in Western countries. Moreover, medicine at that time offered few cures. By developing professional nursing, a whole new, well-paid occupation could be provided women who needed to earn their living.

Nightingale totally rejected the double sexual standard so prevalent in her time. That is, she refused to believe that men and women were fundamentally different in their sexual drives, so that men had to have other women if deprived of their wives, the army's excuse for condoning prostitution. The two sexes had the same moral responsibilities, she held, and a common moral nature.

Yet Nightingale was often critical of women. She felt that women did not take up the opportunities they had, notably in nursing. She began her post-Crimea work with a dedicated band of male collaborators, but no women. Nightingale complained that women did not know the names of Cabinet ministers, the ranks in the army or which churches had bishops, all of which information was available in reference books. She decried women's desire for *love*, to be loved that is, but failure at *sympathy*, the ability to feel with others.

When Nightingale complained in 1861 that she had left no school behind her, that her work had taken no hold among women, she

was stating the simple truth – but speaking too soon. The only particularly worthy women she knew then were not collaborators in the
way Drs Sutherland and Farr, the water engineer Robert Rawlinson
and sanitary expert Edwin Chadwick were. Women friends and relatives helped and sympathized, but did not strategize: family friends
Selina Bracebridge and Mary Clarke Mohl; the 'madre', Laure de Ste
Colombe, who advised her in Rome; her cousin, artist Hilary Bonham
Carter; friend and colleague Dr Elizabeth Blackwel; the 'Reverend
Mother' Mary Clare Moore with whom she nursed in the Crimean
War; and author Harriet Martineau. In time there would be many
women, especially nursing leaders, whom she respected and with
whom she worked closely. Her vision of nursing was always as a
woman-led profession.

Nightingale's exasperation in working with Dr Sutherland appears
throughout their lengthy exchange of notes. Not so well known is the
close and warm relationship she developed with his wife, 'the best of
all my wives', as Nightingale described her. A letter late in life from
Mrs Sutherland recalls 'how deeply and truly I feel all your love and
kindnesses from the first hour we met until now. God bless you always
and return all your loving thoughtfulnesses a thousand-fold onto
your own head, blessings in being blessed'. It closes with 'ever your
affectionate and grateful'.

In the Franco-Prussian War Nightingale was deeply impressed
by the relief work done by Caroline Werckner (to whom she left
money in her will). By the Egyptian and South African campaigns
of the 1880s there was Amy Hawthorn, who was willing to expose
injustices and able to write reports for inquiries. Later still we will
see Nightingale advising her friend, historian Alice Stopford Green,
on her candidacy to become mistress of Girton College, Cambridge.
She supported the work of Anne Jemima Clough in girls' education
and later in the founding of Newnham College, Cambridge. She
assisted Jane (Mrs Nassau) Senior on her appointment as the first
woman Poor Law inspector. Senior was a social reformer who shared

Nightingale's views, in contrast with her political economist husband, Nassau Senior.

Nightingale's relationship with Adeline Paulina Irby was fraught with frustration, for Irby was not a lover of facts, yet Nightingale had enormous respect for her courage and daring in organizing Bosnian relief (to which she contributed herself, and she left Irby money in her will). Nightingale esteemed the philanthropist Octavia Hill, for her work on improving housing for the poor.

Within her own family in earlier years she saw talents being wasted (especially in her artist cousin Hilary Bonham Carter). Later women family members would be dedicated and competent, beginning with Emily Verney in the Franco-Prussian War, Margaret Verney in rural health schemes, and Rosalind Shore Smith, who went to Girton College and worked with her husband in the co-operative movement. Nightingale's relationships with women show an enormous range not only in emotional tone but practical collaboration. She became mentor and friend to two generations of nurses, including Americans, Canadians and Europeans. Correspondence over time shows her increasingly seeking information from them. Yet she was always the moral leader, to whom they went for advice and comfort in trouble.

Nightingale's views on the admission of women to the medical profession were nuanced. In 1859 she arranged an introduction for Elizabeth Blackwell to an eminent doctor to advise her on her career. Later in life Nightingale publicly supported the admission of women to medicine. Yet she was cautious about Elizabeth Blackwell's sister, Emily Blackwell, becoming the first woman doctor in England, because she understood what pressure the first woman would be under, and what sacrifices she would have to make so as not to harm the cause. In 1877 Nightingale wrote the dean of the School of Medicine at London University supporting the admission of women. Still, she would have preferred a different kind of training for women physicians, centred on midwifery and hospitals specializing in the care of women and children.

The Nightingale School sent a matron and trained nurses when the new Hospital for Women was established, the leading force being Elizabeth Garrett Anderson. Nightingale herself subscribed £50 to the building fund. On Garrett Anderson's death it was renamed in her honour.

Nightingale was well aware of the particular need for women doctors in India, where custom forbade women from being examined by a male doctor. Acutely ill women died rather than break this stricture. Nightingale supported endeavours to provide female medical aid to Indian women, notably through what became known as 'the Lady Dufferin Fund', technically the National Association for Supplying Medical Aid to the Women of India. Queen Victoria herself had commissioned Lady Dufferin, wife of the viceroy, to take on this task.

Nightingale promoted the work of the first British woman doctor to practise in India, Dr Mary Scharlieb, who had trained in Madras (now Chennai) initially (she was there with her husband), then in London and Vienna.

Nightingale's last doctor for her own care was a woman, Dr May Thorne, and her death certificate was signed by another woman doctor, Louisa Garrett Anderson, daughter of Elizabeth Garrett Anderson.

Nightingale's views on prostitution and prostitutes were unusual for her time and for ours. She was conventional in regarding prostitution as immoral and she supported 'rescue work' – that is, the attempt to get women prostitutes out of the business. Yet she did not regard sexual immorality as a grave sin (incompetence and indifference on the part of senior administrators were much worse). She was interested in the factors that prompted women to become prostitutes, including both abuse in the home and economic pressures. In her years of struggle against the compulsory inspection and treatment of prostitutes Nightingale would suggest the alternative of going after the pimps.

Nightingale was aware at least by 1860 that syphilis reduced the army's effective numbers. In 1862 she learned the War Office was moving towards legislation for the inspection and compulsory treatment of suspected women prostitutes. She did the first, behind-the-scenes, work to try to prevent it. But the Contagious Diseases Act was adopted in 1864, and subsequently extended.[39] She recruited Harriet Martineau to publicize arguments against the legislation in the liberal *Daily News*, to counter the favourable coverage in the conservative *The Times*. A petition published 31 December 1869 in the *Daily News* launched the movement for repeal. Nightingale and Martineau were the first to sign, followed by Josephine Butler, who then took on the leadership of the repeal movement. It was successful only in 1886. Nightingale played a (discreet) supportive role in those years, and in the international campaign for repeal.

SUGGESTIONS FOR THOUGHT

What an existence is ascribed to God! Always weighing and
balancing our sins against our disadvantages . . . Who
would wish to have such a God?
What a weary life God must have of it![40]
Can it be pleasing to God that man should be
continually praising Him?[41]

Nightingale's three-volume *Suggestions for Thought* has for over a century fascinated its readers, from the few who were permitted to read it during her lifetime to the large number who read excerpts published from it later. The initial writing dates from 1852, that bleak period of her life when she was not permitted to work, so many years after her 'call to service' in 1837. She finished the drafting in 1858–60 and had it printed, in three bulky volumes, in 1860.

Suggestions for Thought has four themes treated at length. First, there is Nightingale's conceptualization of a perfect, just, wise and benevolent God, against the typical portrayal of her own church, and others, as vengeful, angry and punitive, hence unjust and far from perfect. The British working class had largely abandoned the church and any belief in God, Nightingale thought, because of this portrayal. Only with the teaching of a just and loving God, she believed, could they be brought back. The readership she sought was the skilled working class, or 'artizans', as she called them. That they were the prime target is clear in the original title: *Suggestions for Thought to the Searchers after Truth among the Artizans of England*. At John Stuart Mill's suggestion this was revised for volumes 2 and 3 to *Suggestions for Thought to Searchers after Religious Truth*, with no mention of 'artizans'.

That workers seldom attended church was clear in census returns, which Nightingale cited. Some had taken up the 'religion of human-ity' of Auguste Comte, but she rejected that, although she approved of Comte's positivism in science. The solution, she thought, was to present a worthy, attractive God, stripped of the superstitions, miracles and wrath, a God of love who invites humankind to share in making life better.

The second theme is a comparison between the Roman Catholic Church and her own Church of England, all to the favour of the for-mer. The Roman Catholic Church at least made serious demands on its adherents, which her own church did not. It also, perhaps for that reason, was successfully converting disillusioned Anglicans, including some of Nightingale's own friends and acquaintances. Yet the Catholic Church was faulty for its demand for unthinking acceptance of its doctrines, on the basis of its authority, not reason. Both churches taught miracles that never happened, in her view. The Roman Catholic Church even added such miracles as Jesus' house in Nazareth flying to Loretto, in Italy, where it is still a shrine. The Roman Catholic Church also came in for criticism for its excessive demands for humility, self-denial and self-mortification, especially in its religious orders. She was appalled at the teaching of most churches of eternal hellfire for unbaptized infants, who could not help being born.

The third great theme is the oppression of women of her class, the educated and privileged women of Britain who could contribute so much to human betterment, if allowed to use their talents. Instead they were confined to boring, if luxurious, lives within the confines of their family and its narrow acquaintance. Marriage was the only escape for the daughter of the family, and that chancy given her lack of rights in marriage and the narrow range of prospective husbands available to her. Several parts of *Suggestions for Thought* detail this stifling life, notably the essay 'On the theory of daughters' and the better known outburst 'Cassandra'. None of this impassioned writing deals with the plight of women in general, or working-class women, the great majority of the population, although Nightingale would later give much time and thought to improving their condition. *Suggestions for Thought*, rather, is highly personal.

The fourth theme draws on the previous three, to assert that all people are called on, indeed intended, to act with God for the betterment of the world. Nightingale's profound democratic instincts show here, for God included people of every level of society and education. All could contribute to making life better, to people the earth with 'saints', as she put it. That most people lived desperate and unhappy lives, she fully realized. This led to a philosophical defence of her belief in an active eternal life – for the misery of this world could not be the intention of a just God. Only with the possibility of growth, change and happiness in the hereafter could God's justice be reconciled with the brutal facts of the actual life of the vast majority of the world's people.

Nightingale's fierce egalitarianism would inform all her later work on health care. In Chapter 5 her vision of the same high quality of care for the 'sick poor' as provided the best-off patient will be shown. Her aim of replacing the wretched workhouses with non-punitive care facilities for the aged and chronically ill similarly reflects this democratic understanding, theoretically forecast in *Suggestions for Thought*.

While the printed text is in the form of a heavy, third-person philosophical discussion, earlier manuscripts show quite a different approach. There are two draft novels on the plight of women of her class, both rewritten to remove the dialogue and names of characters, keeping the heroines' ideas. Neither novel form worked – both were too talky. The exchanges were laboured and the adjectives excessive, a far cry from the adventure stories Nightingale loved. Yet whatever one might think of the novel-of-ideas style, its desperate message comes across with force.

In one novel draft the main characters are the three earnest daughters of a wealthy, leisured, family like Nightingale's own. They had conflicting theological views, and suitably dramatic names: Portia, Columba and Fulgentia. In the second, shorter, novel form there are only two characters, the tragic Nofariari and her brother Fariseo, who tells her story after her death at age 30. This latter story was the original version of what became 'Cassandra', the best-known part of *Suggestions for Thought*.

There are flights of fancy, beautiful maidens, magicians, an enchantress and phantoms in the novel drafts. Romantic, Italian, settings are described, presumably drawn from Nightingale's own visits to Italy. Images from Renaissance art are used. We see, in short, quite a different side of Nightingale from the prosaic nurse, statistician, social reformer and administrator.

For both draft novels Nightingale removed all the speeches and flowery descriptions when she had the text printed. The quotation marks and characters' names went. 'Portia said', 'dear Fulgentia, you say', became 'It is said', etc. The lavish settings in the manuscript do not appear in the printed *Suggestions* at all. Even the name 'Cassandra', initially a mere 'Aunt Cassandra' in the family novel form, in the printed text appears only in sidebars and headings, not the main text.

Nightingale also used dialogue for the presentation of her theological views. Now, instead of a novel, the characters are real figures, but with entirely fictional speeches: Jacob Abbott (for evangelical Protestantism), Ignatius of Loyola (Roman Catholicism), and Harriet Martineau (agnosticism, but who had been Unitarian). There are shorter appearances of the poet Percy Bysshe Shelley (or more precisely his 'Queen Mab: a philosophical poem') and Protestant reformer John

Calvin. Auguste Comte was not a character, but his views were much quoted in *Suggestions for Thought*. But the main contender in the dialogue is an unnamed 'M. S.', who is probably Nightingale's aunt, Mary Smith, with whom she collaborated on the writing. As a result, it is not clear how much Nightingale herself was speaking on any theological point, or how much her more heterodox aunt. Certainly Nightingale's later views left behind many ideas firmly asserted by M. S. as evident to the rational mind. Most of what Nightingale said about God to nurses she would have condemned in *Suggestions for Thought*.

NIGHTINGALE'S DEFENCE OF GOD

To Nightingale the core teaching of Christianity made God out to be unjust and vengeful. It laid it down 'as an absolute truth' that God's scheme 'was the creation of a vast number of beings, called into existence without any will of their own', the fate of 'the greater number . . . to be everlasting misery, of the lesser number eternal happiness'.

She did not see people's time on earth as a trial, to determine whether they would go to heaven or hell in the hereafter, nor that the afterlife would be mere absorption into God: 'Can we suppose that God sent forth a being to suffer and struggle, merely in order that it should be re-absorbed into God's existence? Most lame and impotent conclusion. Why send it forth? To what end its suffering?' She thought that God intended all people to come to perfection, in time or eternity. Otherwise the suffering would not be justifiable. 'By God's will and law, *no* man can exist without being on the road to perfection.'

Eternal punishment could only come from 'revenge', not 'justice', Nightingale affirmed, and so could not be the will of a just God. 'It seems strange that under *any* interpretation of the rule of the Being whom we call perfect, it should be supposed that an eternity of suffering is destined for beings whom it cannot benefit.'

Nor could a perfect God be vain. The 'worship' of God went back to 'Oriental despotism', Nightingale said. Rather we should seek to serve

God, and this 'from sympathy and understanding, not from blind obedience'. We should not be in 'servile subjection to Him, crawling before Him'. 'Can it be pleasing to God that man should be always praising Him? Can it be satisfactory to Him to hear us continually saying, how good Thou art, how great Thou art . . . It can be only flattery.'

Nightingale railed against belief in miracles in many places in *Suggestions for Thought*. It was not a question of evidence, for 'no evidence could convince us of them'. Some people wanted to believe in them, thinking they found God in them, but 'we should lose our God, if we were to find Him performing miracles'. How could we have 'sympathy' with and 'esteem' the God 'who carries about houses in the night', referring to the miracle of Loretto, 'and opens and shuts a picture's eyes', referring to a recent miracle of a statue in Rimini, Italy.

Logically, Nightingale did not think that people should have to pray for the things that God knew they needed. 'If my having a safe voyage to America depended on my prayer to Omnipotence, I should not revere the Omnipotent.' A manuscript source explains, that 'our God always does what is wise, whether we suggest it to Him or no'.

ROMAN CATHOLICISM AND PROTESTANTISM

Nightingale had a strong appreciation of the Roman Catholic religious orders for their serious attempt to act out the gospel message. But she faulted them for their stress on self-mortification. There should be less emphasis on 'turning away from evil, but taking means to feel and think and do what is good'. 'If we are thinking of "self-mortification", we are thinking of ourselves, whom we had better forget; it is in itself a kind of self-seeking.' 'To do the work of God and mankind is the highest work.'

The Catholic orders laid down rules, even that monks and nuns should have an 'equal love' to all, and 'to give up their own opinion and judgment for that of another, to wish to be accounted fools'. Better to have a realistic assessment of one's abilities, she thought.

On the practice of confession Nightingale, at this time – not later – found much to commend in Roman Catholicism. Her own church was 'so like John Bull, so business-like, so brief and terse'. It asked: 'Have you done all that is wrong? Well, then, say you are sorry, and we will absolve you; we have no time to hear what for'. The Church of Rome made people go over them 'one by one'. 'John Bull will have plenty for his money. He will have his services long, till he is quite tired, that he may have his money's worth, like his concerts, plenty in them, no cheating, till he goes home yawning. So he has his confession, "*lumping*" all his sins together, and then his absolution, and then his praise, and then his litany, asking for every imaginable thing, and ending with asking God for "mercy on *all* men", lest he should have left out anything, till there does not remain to God the smallest choice or judgment.'[42]

Obedience for the sake of obedience was offensive to Nightingale, yet in a great undertaking obedience was required to ensure its success – perhaps even the survival of its members. But the kind of obedience required in a religious order was to check people's idiosyncrasies, which went against human nature. On nursing practice Nightingale would make much of the concept of 'intelligent obedience' to doctor's orders – which most decidedly did not mean blind obedience.

Whether Roman Catholic or Anglican, religious orders generally had 'one powerful mind at the head, and a great many childish minds under him (or her)'. If another powerful mind came in among the subordinates, it ended by that one 'being expelled, expelling, or becoming stupified'. Religious orders did not make progress. 'Great minds found them; little minds spring out of them. There is scarcely a historical instance of a discoverer, an inventor, a genius or a benefactor of mankind being produced by a religious order *after* it is once compact and established.'

In one fictional debate St Ignatius of Loyola defended the authority of the Roman Catholic Church, while M. S. argued for human reason and direct connection with God.[43] St Ignatius asked how one could know that his reason, feeling and conscience told him the truth. M. S. conceded that we would see falsely with a diseased eye, so that 'we must take care to keep our sources of information in a healthy state'. Not convinced, St Ignatius pointedly asked: 'Then you believe in no inspiration, no atonement, and no Christ?' M. S. replied with quite a different view of the doctrine of atonement. 'Christ indeed came into the world to save sinners, to wash them in his blood. To deliver man from sin and its consequences, to establish the kingdom of heaven within him, to at-one him with God were truly Christ's mission and that of many more upon the earth. These things will be attained and would not have been attained without Christ.'

The Protestant Jacob Abbott asked M. S. if she was a Unitarian. M. S. replied that 'the Unitarians say that no man is divine, none an incarnation of God, the Trinitarians that there was one'. She argued that 'all are divine' in that 'all are incarnations of Him, and receive inspiration from Him'. Thus the Trinitarian view was a 'truer doctrine' than the Unitarian.[44]

St Ignatius protested M. S.'s rejection of the church's authority: 'Oh! to be as you are without authority for a faith! I would not be in such a condition, no, not for worlds'. M. S. merely agreed that it was 'dreadful' for Roman Catholics to be without authority. 'But we *have* authority. Do you call God Himself authority? We are but the vessels. He fills them and we must keep the vessels unsoiled and pure'. The debate carried on, St Ignatius continuing to argue the need for the church to decide for people, M. S. disagreeing.

While Nightingale decried the Roman Catholic Church's insistence on authority, for the right of all to use their reason, she firmly objected to the usual liberal defence of 'private judgment'. It showed how irrelevant most people thought religion was. 'Far be it from us to allow any man to construct a railroad from north to south as he pleases', she fumed. But in these (so-called) '*liberal* days, the tolerance (what a word!) is admired which lets every man construct the road from earth to heaven as he pleases.'[45]

Nightingale had particularly disparaging views about the privileged status of her church's rich bishops. While the disciples 'went about as beggars, doing good', and hermits 'lived in holes in the rocks, doing nothing', her church's bishops 'drove about with servants in purple liveries behind their carriages. But these cannot all be Christianity'.[46]

It was a sore point for Nightingale that the Roman Catholic Church, with its wrong views of miracles (even worse than her own), should prompt so much enthusiasm. Her fervent belief in the God of law was a hard sell. Like a book of science, her God was 'all order and beauty and goodness, and He excites no feeling'. St Teresa's God was 'all injustice and disorder', yet 'we find her in a rapture about Him'. 'The God of law is always speaking to us – always saying what is wise and good. The God of St Teresa speaks to her sometimes, and says something which is often foolish and not good. Curious indeed, that while the God of science never appears to have excited any feeling, the other God has excited so much!'[47]

THE OPPRESSION OF EDUCATED WOMEN

In *Suggestions for Thought* Nightingale showed how women were forced to become hypocritical. In her view, 'suffering' would be better than 'indifferentism', *pain* better than *paralysis*. Better to die struggling in the breakers seeking a new world than to stand idly on the shore. Yet the actual life of a woman of Nightingale's genteel class was spent not on 'high ideas and generous feelings', but in sympathy given and received for a dinner, a piece of furniture, a well laid out garden and such acts of charity as taking soup to the poor. She suggested that 'the next Christ will perhaps be a female Christ', immediately to ask rhetorically 'But do we see one woman who looks like a female Christ? or even like "the messenger before her face", to go before her and prepare the hearts and minds for her?'

Opportunities for women, marriage and a dedicated single life are major issues throughout *Suggestions for Thought*, not only in

'Cassandra'. The discussion about inheritance is revealing, where one daughter pleads that Fulgentia, the character most like Nightingale, should not have to wait for her parents' deaths to inherit, which might not be until she was 50 or 60. Nightingale in fact was 33 when her father finally gave her an annuity, in 1853 (after the writing of this draft). She was over 50 when he died, nearly 60 when her mother died. Again the printed version makes no mention of her own family.

If there were good reasons for Nightingale not publishing *Suggestions for Thought*, there are even more for not publishing the anguished cry that was 'Cassandra'. It first appeared in print in 1928, as an appendix to Ray Strachey's classic on the English suffrage movement, *'The Cause': A Short History of the Women's Movement in Great Britain*.[48]

There is very little action in the surviving manuscript (how much was destroyed or lost is anybody's guess). At the end of what we do have, Columba, the defender of Roman Catholicism and religious orders, has made her decision – not only to convert to Roman Catholicism but to become a nun, a Sister of Charity, the order with which Nightingale stayed in Paris. The exotic novel ends with the death of Nofariari, which becomes the end also of the printed version.

Two sets of excerpts are given here so that the original and printed versions can be compared. Figure 2.3 comes from the English family novel, Figure 2.4 gives the original ending of 'Cassandra', from the exotic novel.

Figure 2.3 The English family novel

Unpublished manuscript:

My daughter and I were walking together. The high south wind was hurrying by, the sun shining bright and hot in the cloudless heavens, but the air was filled with a fog of dust carried before the gale, which blew ceaselessly, fiercely, like a destiny never weary of suffering – so at least said my poor foolish girl. The dust formed into whirlwinds and whitened all the fresh grass and the yellow spring buds which were coming out. 'So it is with my life', she said. 'The wind has blown down all my supports and hopes and plans. The dust has dried them up. But the sun is still shining high in the heavens and the fresh wind is still blowing.' . . .

'How often I think of our Saviour's temptation', she said. 'It is the epitome of all life. It, as it was no doubt, the epitome of his own, which he told his disciples in that form. A sensitive, noble, spirit could perhaps hardly bear to tell it in that form'. 'But how can you', I said, 'have the experience of our Saviour?'[49]

Printed version:

'Christ's temptation is the epitome of all life, as it was, no doubt, the epitome of his own, which he told to his disciples in that form. A sensitive, noble spirit could perhaps hardly bear to speak of it in any other form'.

Unpublished manuscript:

Three times I have tried to take the great leap. Once, fourteen years ago, when I waited, longed for a man's education at college, and thought of disguising myself and going to Cambridge. Once, seven years ago, when I endeavoured to enter a hospital to learn my profession there, in order afterwards to teach it in a better way. And once, having failed, with all my plans annihilated, I resolved to try marriage with a good man . . .

'And why did you not take one of these leaps, my child?' I said. 'The first I myself had not courage for. The second you, of course, would not suffer – and I gave it up! It cost me my life . . . if by life is meant all spirit, energy, vitality . . . I had thought of it ever since I was six years old. I might have been the [John] Howard of hospitals, which I mention, not, I think, from any puerile vanity now, but merely because I believe, in *that case*, while the vocation would if gratified become the angels' wings to bear me up and I should not have dashed my foot upon the stone. Oh! if I had done it what a different creature I should have been. But you could not tell that. I do not blame'.

Printed version:

Women sometimes try to take the great leap; they long for a man's education at college, and sometimes even think of disguising themselves and going to Cambridge. They endeavour to enter institutions, to learn a charitable profession, in order afterwards to teach it in a better way, or when all other 'trades' fail, they try marriage with a good man, who loves perhaps his wife, but who initiates her into the regular life of the world.

Disappointment often costs the woman her life – if by life is meant all spirit, energy, vitality – while the vocation, if gratified, as often becomes the angel's hand to bear her up, that she shall not dash her foot against the stone.[50]

There are great differences in the final death scene between the novel form and the final printed 'Cassandra'. The explanation for the protagonist's death, given by her narrator brother, was that she was 'wearied of life'. No cause of death is specified in either version, but the original is much fuller and tells who Nofariari and Fariseo were.

Figure 2.4   The original ending of 'Cassandra'[51]

Unpublished version:

Before I go on, I had better tell who 'I' am. My name is Fariseo. I am one of those who are called the cynics of the age, who openly confess their own selfishness, admit the want of the times, and preach that we should bear with those making this confession, not with sorrow of heart nor well-trained resignation, but without shame and without difficulty, as on the whole the best state of mind. I am the brother of poor Nofariari, and I tell her story as she told it me, one day when I blamed her for not finding her happiness in life as I and her contemporaries have done, and she answered that I did not know whether her life had been such that she could either find happiness in it or alter it. I made some few notes of our conversation, for it occurred a short time only before her death. My poor sister! She died at thirty, wearied of life, in which she could do nothing, and having ceased to live the intellectual life long before she was deserted by the physical life. I saw her on her deathbed and, giving way to the tears and exclamations natural on such occasions, was answered by her.

The dying woman to her mourners. 'Oh! If you knew how gladly I leave this life, how much more courage I feel to take the chance of another than of anything I see before me in this, you would put on your wedding clothes instead of mourning for me!' 'But', I said, 'so much talent! so many gifts! such good which you might have done!'

'The world will be put back some little time by my death', she said, 'you see I estimate my powers at least as highly as you can, but it is by the death which has taken place some years ago in me, not by the death which is about to take place now. And so is the world put back by the death of everyone who has to sacrifice the development of his or her own peculiar gifts to conventionality! (which were meant, not for selfish gratification, but for the improvement of that world).' . . .

She lay for some time silent. Then starting up and standing upright, for the first time for many months, she stretched out her arms and cried: 'Free, free, oh! divine freedom, art thou come at last? Welcome, beautiful death!' She fell forward on her face. She was dead. One of her last requests had been that neither name nor date should be placed on her grave. Still less the expression of regret or of admiration, but simply the words, 'I believe in God'.

Printed version:

[sidebar] Cassandra, who can neither find happiness in life, nor alter it, dies.

The dying woman to her mourners, 'Oh! If you knew how gladly I leave this life, how much more courage I feel to take the chance of another, than of anything I see before me in this, you would put on your wedding clothes instead of mourning for me!' 'But', they say, 'so much talent! So many gifts! Such good which you might have done!' . . .

    Cassandra dies. 'Free, free, oh! divine freedom, art thou come at last? Welcome, beautiful death!'

    Let neither name nor date be placed on her grave, still less the expression of regret or of admiration, but simply the words, 'I believe in God'.

GOD SHARES WITH HUMANKIND

Finally, on the last theme, Nightingale firmly believed that God shared His divine attributes with human beings – He did not reserve them for Himself: 'He shares all. Would this benevolence otherwise be perfect, or if it were, would not His power or wisdom be limited?' This is what enabled her to have such a high conception of the possibilities of human endeavour bringing about good.

    Nightingale's idea of a 'theocracy' at first glance startles, but it is part of her idea of God leading people to create a better world. It was a 'sublime idea' of the Jews that they should 'be governed not by kings and presidents but by God!' What a change it would be in England if Cabinet ministers were selected 'for the purpose of discovering and carrying out the purposes of God in politics, for executing the laws of God'.[52]

    Evidently people now thought God 'quite inadequate to carrying on the business of a great nation; a nation would fall to pieces if its business were done according to His will, and no wonder, it certainly would, if done according to what we conceive *now* to be His will, to what we are *told* is His purpose. No wonder we exclude Him from our Cabinet and our politics'.

    Nightingale's view of God oddly puts her in the company of right-wing fundamentalist advocates of 'intelligent design'. Certainly she believed that creation was the work of an intelligent, indeed perfect, just and benevolent Designer. But far from being anti-scientific,

Nightingale was a thorough believer in science, even as the means for realizing God's moral government on earth. Nightingale's politics were always left-of-centre and liberal.

A more idealized role for marriage is part of this new, better way: 'two in one and one in God'. While so much of *Suggestions for Thought* pointed out how bad marriage in fact was for women, a marriage of two persons with a shared calling, to work together with God for this better world, was a possibility: 'Two in one, one in all, all in God.' But while there was joy in marriage, God would not leave the unmarried in a state of starvation. 'There is food in *all* love, sympathy, benevolence, search for truth, patient trust, in all righteous exercise of the faculties.' Marriage was not essential for a woman's happiness, Nightingale believed. Moreover, Christ was her example: he had lived fully without marrying or feeling a necessity to.

NOTES ON MATTERS

AFFECTING THE

HEALTH, EFFICIENCY, AND HOSPITAL ADMINISTRATION

OF THE

BRITISH ARMY,

FOUNDED CHIEFLY ON THE EXPERIENCE OF THE LATE WAR

BY

FLORENCE NIGHTINGALE

Presented by request to the Secretary of State for War.

LONDON:
PRINTED BY HARRISON AND SONS, ST. MARTIN'S LANE, W.C.
1858.

3. Facsimile title page of Nightingale's 'confidential report', *Notes on the Health of the British Army.*

War

It was entirely unplanned that Nightingale should become famous as a war nurse, and then spend so much of her life concerned with army matters. Her 'call to service' was to save lives, and she would have begun in civilian hospitals, if she had been allowed to. It happened that the Crimean War was her opportunity to serve, and she took it. She then used her status as a heroine to effect many other reforms, notably for the 'sick poor'. Naturally she continued to work for better care for ordinary soldiers, who were themselves, when ill, the 'sick poor'.

Nightingale joked about being a long time employee of the War Office, but she early came to understand the horrors of war. Her practical work in the Crimean War is the first topic here, but, as later wars are considered, her interest in militarism and the causes of war emerges.

THE CRIMEAN WAR

The Barrack Hospital before Nightingale's arrival:
There were very few beds . . . the poor soldiers were brought
down with scarcely any clothes, their clothes having been worn
off their backs, [they] were placed upon palliasses [mats], and
their clothes, or at least the remnants of them, [were] full of
vermin . . . no washing had been performed in the hospital, nor
the floor washed for six weeks . . . no washing of linen had been
performed . . . there were no hospital dresses . . . neither cooking,
nor comforts of any kind provided . . . the whole state of the
hospital . . . was pestiferous and infectious, the privies being in
such a state that nobody could approach the place.[1]

4. Florence Nightingale statue at the Crimean War Memorial, Waterloo
Place, London. Photograph courtesy of Marilyn Greaves.

The Crimean War[2] was a shabby affair if its motives and results are
considered. It was a glorious war if acts of personal heroism and gal-
lantry count. That the British, French and Turks won at all is largely
attributed to the greater number of crucial errors made by Russian
generals. The infamous 'charge of the Light Brigade', on 25 October
1854, resulted in the loss of almost an entire British brigade, but the
battle was won when the Russians failed to take advantage of British
mistakes.

The British Isles are situated far from the Crimean peninsula in
the Black Sea. The ostensible issues at stake in the war included the

status of Orthodox Church members in Muslim Turkey and control over certain churches in the Holy Land. The underlying, real, motive was Russian expansion in the Balkans. In 1853 Russia took over some territory south of the Danube. It seemed to the British and French likely that it would go farther West and South, possibly even taking Constantinople, if not forcibly stopped. In fact the landing of British and French troops in Bulgaria resulted in the Russians withdrawing north of the Danube.

Russia at the time was an absolutist tsardom. Serfdom was still the lot of millions and the rights and liberties enjoyed by Britons and, to a lesser extent, other Europeans, were nowhere in sight. Nightingale's friend Harriet Martineau justified British participation in the war on grounds of Russian tyranny, language which Nightingale also used. Yet Turkey was no more a democracy than was Russia, and even had slavery. Nightingale herself never said that the Crimean War was a just war. It seems that she never struggled with the just-war concept or its application in any particular war. Wars were an unhappy fact of life, and someone had to look after the wounded and sick that resulted from them.

In a letter late in life, Nightingale attributed the Crimean War to 'the marching of Russia in to subdue Hungary (in 1848)'. This made the people of England so furious with Russia that they went to war in 1854, not over the ostensible causes, the 'holy places', but 'it was our rage with Russia that brought about the Crimean War'. The context here is that good can come out of evil, even that the Crimean War 'brought about the reform of nursing'.

The British Army had not fought a war in more than 40 years, other than expeditions against ill-equipped forces to expand its empire, and it was badly unprepared for this one. Large numbers died, although probably not more proportionately than in the Napoleonic Wars. The Crimean War, however, was the first one with war correspondents reporting by telegraph, and photographers as well as war artists. *The Times* correspondent in London drew the unsavoury comparison of the lack of women nurses aiding the British sick and wounded compared with their French allies, who had Sisters of Charity. The Russians, about whom less was known, also had nursing sisters, organized by the Grand Duchess Helena. The War Office, in its preparations for the war, had considered sending women nurses, but rejected the idea as too radical. *The Times* asked why Britain had no Sisters of Charity.

Nightingale had already made her own decision to go to nurse in the war when she was asked officially, by the secretary of state at war, Sidney Herbert, to lead a team of nurses there. (She knew the Herberts from her time in Rome 1847–48, and Elizabeth Herbert was a member of the ladies' committee of the Establishment for Gentlewomen during Illness, where she was then superintendent.) The arrangements were made in days, her friends interviewing applicants while she organized supplies and met with officials. Nightingale had been assured that the army was well supplied, but she took the precaution of acquiring food, medical supplies, linen, clothing and other basic items in Marseilles en route. *The Times* collected £7,000, which it put to her disposal, and which proved to be enormously helpful. Of more dubious help, people sent gifts in kind, of food, clothing, bandages, books, etc., all of which had to be acknowledged and put to use.

Nightingale and her nurses landed at Scutari, on the Asian side of the Bosphorus, across from Constantinople, on 5 November 1854, the same day the Battle of Inkermann was fought in the Crimea. Sick and wounded troops were only just arriving from the previous battle, fought at Balaclava on 25 October 1854. Large numbers of deaths had already occurred, especially from cholera and other bowel diseases, in the camps near Varna in the summer weeks they were there. Both the British and French suffered enormously. The French commander indeed died of cholera in October. The troops were also suffering from malnutrition (which would get worse in the winter in the trenches). Soldiers had died on board ship sailing to the Crimea, and on the march, before a shot was fired. The men were so weak they were ordered to leave behind their kits, which in fact were never replaced. This decision, too, led to enormous suffering as cold set in, as will be seen in the excerpts in Figure 3.1.

On arrival in Scutari the nurses found the army atrociously under-equipped medically and lacking in all kinds of essentials, including food and bedding. The wounded were brought by boat, the journey itself taking days. Many men died during transport or immediately on arrival. The barracks provided to the British by the Turkish Government for their hospital in Scutari had been built over an open sewer. There was a central courtyard, which prevented the bad air from escaping, and no cross-ventilation. The space available to each patient was one-quarter the normal. All this was known by the senior administrators at the War Office and the Army Medical Department, but not then by Nightingale. A major purpose of the confidential report she wrote after the war was to set down precisely who reported on urgent problems and when, and who delayed or failed to act at all.

Nightingale did hands-on work as well as the administration. She assisted at amputations and attended the ill. Her night-time walks through the wards gave rise to the image of 'the lady with the lamp'. She provided clean bedding and clothing, good food (and brandy) to the sick and wounded. She wrote letters for dying soldiers and advised their families of deaths. She instituted a banking system whereby soldiers could send their earnings home. She established the first healthy leisure outlets for ordinary soldiers, 'reading rooms' with cards and magazines, when alcohol was otherwise the only option. She set up the 'Inkerman Café', a coffee house for soldiers. She enlisted the assistance of an Anglican priest and his wife to help the wives and partners who were left behind at Scutari when the men left for the war zone – they were outside her jurisdiction.

Nightingale's nursing establishment began with the 38 nurses who had travelled with her to Scutari. A further contingent of 47 arrived in December 1854, sent without Nightingale's knowledge, which caused a row over her authority and practical problems (there was no space to house them). Nor had the doctors been consulted on an increase in numbers, and some wanted no nurses at all. The group was dispersed to other hospitals, but tensions remained. The superior of the Irish Sisters of Mercy in this group, unlike that of the Bermondsey group, refused to recognize Nightingale's authority, although she had signed a contract on behalf of all her nuns to do so.

Some of the doctors never accepted the presence of Nightingale and her nurses; others soon learned that going to her was the way to get things done. She had supplies that the army either did not have, or did not know that it had because its record keeping was so bad. This would be the pattern throughout Nightingale's long career of reorganizing society: there were supporters and collaborators on change, opponents and upholders of the status quo. The nurses themselves, at Nightingale's insistence, worked solely under the direction of the doctors.

Most of the soldiers' deaths in hospital were from disease, not bullets, a point Nightingale and her team would stress in all their reform work after the war: 19,000 from illness (mainly infectious diseases), 4,000 from wounds. Nightingale regarded the deaths from illness as unnecessary – anything above the 'normal death rate' was.

Mortality remained high Nightingale's first winter at the Barrack Hospital, despite the institution of better nutrition, cleaning and nursing. The killer was the hospital's defective sewers, toilets and ventilation. Not until the sanitary commission sent out from England arrived in March 1855, and major structural re-engineering done, was the death rate brought down. By the end of the war, the mortality rate from illness was no greater than that of a comparable population in England – men in the industrial city of Manchester.

It has become fashionable to blame Nightingale for the failures at the Barrack Hospital at Scutari. Author Hugh Small did, and even argued that she blamed herself, indeed that her guilt was so great as to make her ill. A BBC broadcast in 2008 echoed this bizarre construction of events. At the least it is to shoot the messenger for the bad news, for it was her analysis that demonstrated what went wrong, with citations from official documents.

As early as August 1854 Lord Raglan gave instructions for the 'purification' of the Scutari barrack for its use as a hospital for the sick and wounded (it had been used in the spring simply as a barrack, before the troops were sent on to Varna). No such preparation was done. Dr Hall inspected the hospital once, in October 1854, sent back a glowing report, and never went back to reinspect, even as deaths mounted terribly. Nightingale would argue that the deaths need not have occurred if the hospital had been properly cleaned, or at least if strenuous action had been taken when problems were reported. One might also ask who decided on a hospital at distant Scutari at all, requiring the transport of wounded and sick across the Black Sea?

Hugh Small faulted Nightingale further for not collecting data herself on the deaths when they began to rise in November 1854, although she had neither the mandate nor the means to do so. She later found out that the army had been collecting data, but evidently not using it for practical purposes. Getting responsible authorities to make use of the data already in their hands would be a lesson she learned from the Crimean War. References to this appear as late as 1890.

Nightingale herself nearly died during the war. She came down with 'Crimean fever', then thought to be a form of typhus; some of her nurses died of it. Nightingale of course recovered, but it has been suggested that she returned to England with chronic brucellosis.[3] Again, detractors would make Nightingale out to have been a malingerer, or a 'nervous breakdown' case. Small himself referred to her 'illness' in quotation marks.

A peace treaty was signed in Paris on 30 March 1856 and Nightingale left Scutari for England on 28 July, after the last soldiers had been sent home. She sailed with her Aunt Mai Smith via Athens and Marseilles, declining the offer of a man-o'-war to bring her home. They stayed overnight in Paris and took a train to London. The incognito return shows Nightingale's extreme abhorrence of personal publicity – she travelled as 'Miss Smith', with her aunt. In London she called on the Sisters of Mercy with whom she had worked in Scutari, at their convent in Bermondsey. She then took the train to Derbyshire and arrived on foot at Lea Hurst late on 7 August 1856.

Nightingale returned to England a national heroine. Her soldiers and their families would be ever grateful – her feats were widely reported in the press. Now a celebrity, she declined the numerous invitations of the rich, noble and famous. She decided to ask nothing for herself, but to devote her political capital to argue for basic reforms. This gave her great power in the negotiations to follow, when she sought a royal commission to investigate the causes of the deplorable conditions and massive deaths suffered by the British Army in the East.

A fund had been raised mid-war (1855) in her honour, close to £45,000 (worth US$3 million today), and the Nightingale Trust established to run it. Nightingale eventually settled on two main projects: the creation of the first non-sectarian training school for nurses, at St Thomas' Hospital, and a midwifery nursing training programme, at King's College Hospital (both hospitals in London). They began in 1860 and 1861, respectively.

Nightingale's first priority was the analysis of what went wrong in the war itself. She worked with a team of experts, some of whom became collaborators for decades thereafter: Drs Sutherland, Farr and Sir John McNeill and engineer Robert Rawlinson. She did two parallel pieces of analysis, one for the official royal commission report, the other a confidential 'précis' requested by Lord Panmure, the Secretary of State for War, but which turned out to be the 900-page *Notes on the Health of the British Army*, as it is abbreviated here. (The full title is *Notes on Matters Affecting the Health, Efficiency and Hospital Administration of the British Army Founded Chiefly on the Experience of the Late War*.) Both reports were finished in 1858, the official report published by the government, the misnamed 'précis' privately printed, paid for by herself and sent confidentially to trusted persons.

The royal commission report and her own 'Confidential report' overlap considerably, but the two had quite distinct purposes and were in commensurately different styles. The official report was positive, constructive and future oriented. The mistakes of the past were treated briskly and no blame was laid on particular individuals. The longer *Notes on the Health of the British Army* is much more comprehensive. It too looked forward, but after comprehensive and detailed analysis of what went wrong and who was to blame for it. Reports of critical lacks in the field are carefully documented. Lack of action and delays were also noted, with names and dates. It forcefully showed that doctors in the field had told their superiors at the Army Medical Department what was wrong. They had described the miserable conditions the soldiers had to endure in the trenches and urged that supplies be sent. They reported on the overflowing sewers and toilets at the Barrack Hospital. Soldiers suffered and died as a result of the failure to act on these gross sanitary defects. Both reports had recommendations regarding regular, civilian hospitals. All the material for both reports came from the records of the army itself.

The Queen's invitation to Nightingale to visit at Balmoral Castle gave Nightingale the opportunity to argue for a royal commission on the war. Her team of experts briefed her on the best method to convince Lord Panmure, Secretary of State for War, who would also be at Balmoral. Opposing them were the officials who ran the Army Medical Department, whose lack of preparation and poor adminis-tration would be chief subjects of investigation. Nightingale spent a month at Birk Hall, then the home of the Queen's physician, Sir James Clark, near Balmoral Castle. She stopped several days in Edinburgh en route for briefing by Sir John McNeill. The strategy worked, a royal commission was agreed on, the members were almost all to their liking and the terms of reference most satisfactory. Nightingale was the key player on all the stages of the royal commission, from its establishment, choice of members and terms of reference, through the conduct of its work. She undertook such tasks as preparing witnesses.

Nightingale had a tough three-hour bargaining session with Lord
Panmure, 'my Pan', as she called him, to get the members of the royal
commission she and her team wanted. Her notes record that he wrote
down a list in three categories of three each: army doctors, civil doctors and the 'jury', with Sidney Herbert at the head.[4] She regretted
that Panmure would not bring back Thomas Alexander from Canada,
but in fact Herbert made it a condition of his accepting the chair that
Alexander be appointed. She explained that Panmure had insisted
on three army doctors, 'so, like a sensible general in retreat I named
Brown, surgeon major, Grenadier Guards, therefore not wedded to
Dr Smith . . . left Lord P. his Mclachlan, who will do less harm than a
better man'. Panmure 'generously struck out' the name of the purveyor
Nightingale thought incompetent, Mr Milton, so she 'was so good as
to leave him Dr Smith, the more so as I could not help it'. 'Pan' was
'amazed at my condescension' in allowing a military doctor, Balfour,
as the secretary, 'so I concealed the fact of the man being a dangerous
animal and obstinate innovator'.

Other comments show that Nightingale won what she wanted on
terms of reference for the commission, but lost on some hoped-for
immediate improvements. An important concession to her: 'Sir J. Hall
not to be director general while Lord P. in office – I won'. (Her favourite, Thomas Alexander, got the top post after Smith's retirement.)

There were delays. Lord Panmure, the War Secretary, also known as
'the bison', required months more lobbying before the royal commission
was actually announced. The team, however, used this delay to prepare
their own material. The commission was then able to work quickly,
issuing its report several months after its official appointment.

In 1857, still in the course of doing the research for the two reports,
Nightingale wrote Baron von Bunsen, former Prussian ambassador to
the UK, and a family friend who had early on encouraged her to pursue her call to nursing. The letter, excerpted in Figure 3.1, shows how
desperate she felt about the need for fundamental reform in the care
of the sick and wounded in war, and how frustrated she was by what

seemed to be inaction on the part of the British Government. In fact, it did subsequently act on most of the recommendations of the royal commission report, including the creation of the Barrack and Hospital Improvement Commission (which managed improvements over the next decades), the Army Medical School (to teach sanitary science), a statistical department (to track disease and enable swift responses to epidemics) and a cooking school (to improve nutrition). But all that took time. The letter serves also to underscore Nightingale's clear determination to specify responsibility for the war disaster.

Figure 3.1 Letter on failure to learn from the Crimean War[5]

---

24 February 1857

Since I came home, I have had work far more constant, more absorbing, more heart-rending than even in the Crimea . . .

Our government is quite determined to do nothing. Of that, everyone is now persuaded – nothing, I mean, to prevent another army, under the same circumstances, being destroyed as the last was. Everyone is well aware that, if war were to break out tomorrow, we should have the whole scene of '54 over again.

Those who helped to lose that magnificent army are now careless, at their ease, indifferent or triumphant. Those who helped to save it are cast aside, rejected and despised . . .

They have cut down everything that has to do with the scientific element of the army, the efficiency, morality and health of the soldier. They have left everything which has to do with staff appointments . . .

England is a country which learns by experiments and not by experience, and she has learnt nothing by her colossal calamity.

What that calamity was I believe one must have been in the Crimea to know. The newspapers were *temperate*.

I thought we were making progress. For, ten years ago, they would not have sent out a sanitary commission, nor would a member have got up in the House of Commons and said that the loss of the army was *preventable.*

But, now that the sanitary commission of the army comes home and says that the sanitary condition of the army *at home* is worse than that of the worst parts of London . . .

I shall get out of the government service as soon as I can, and take service in some hospital in London.

Nightingale worked prodigiously assembling statistics, developing, with Dr Farr, 'coxcombs' or pie charts to portray the data graphically. She declined to give evidence in person but did the next best thing by submitting a written document with her answers to the questions put to her (which questions of course she and her team had formulated). This 'Answers to Written Questions' report is remarkable for its pithiness.

Question: To what do you mainly ascribe the mortality in the hospitals?
Answer: To sanitary defects.

She showed that there had been a mortality rate of 60 per cent in the first seven months of the war from disease alone, worse than any cholera epidemic. The reforms brought the mortality rate down below that of troops stationed in England. This revealed the excessive rate of mortality of troops in peacetime conditions, a problem that would soon be addressed. All these points were fleshed out by detailed tables and coloured pie charts.

The royal commission recommendations were directed to putting into place a thoroughly different system. Nightingale then recruited Harriet Martineau to write 'leaders' (comment or op-ed articles) for the *Daily News* featuring their reform line. Martineau also wrote a book, published in 1859, *England and her Soldiers*, to popularize the analysis and recommendations of the royal commission. Nightingale gave her the larger 'précis' as background, but told her not to quote it directly. It is to this more comprehensive report that we turn for the full examination of what went wrong.

NIGHTINGALE'S 'CONFIDENTIAL REPORT'

Nightingale explained in the preface to *Notes on the Health of the British Army* that much of the most crucial information surfaced only as pages of the official report emerged from the press. This was the original correspondence between the director general in London, the principal medical officer at Scutari and medical officers with the troops – 976 letters. The list, with a brief description of the letters, became an appendix of the official report, and she drew on the letters in her 'précis' to show dates of reports of problems and whatever action was taken on them. She added substantial new sections to the précis, as she explained: 'The whole of these letters have been carefully gone over, and they appear to me to throw so much new light on the administrative defects inherent in the present system of the Army Medical Department, and on the causes of the calamities which befell the army during the late war'.

She then prefixed an abstract of the principal documents, not only to confirm the statements she made in the text, but 'to indicate the administrative changes necessary for preventing similar calamities in future, as far as human foresight can do so'. Excerpts on key points show: (1) that the general orders made by Lord Raglan were adequate, but not carried out, leading to the weakened health, malnutrition and exposure of the soldiers, and further that the Army Medical Department failed to flesh out the general orders with specifics; (2) that the defects of the Barrack Hospital at Scutari made for a special case – the result both of inadequate initial inspection and failure to act when actual problems emerged. We begin at (or near) the beginning, the 'sufferings and privations of the army from April 1854' – that is, long before battle began.

Figure 3.2 'Notes on the Sufferings and Privations of the Army'[6]

The army of 25,000 men intended to land in Turkey in April 1854, at some spot to be determined by the position of the Russian Army, was preceded, owing to the foresight of the British Government, by an engineer, three medical and one commissariat officers, to report upon the facilities of the country for their several objects.

It does not appear, however, that the medical officers ever placed themselves in communication with the resident practitioners of the country, with the view of making known to the army medical staff the peculiarities of the effects of the climate in regard to the treatment of diseases . . .

The army landed at Gallipoli, proceeded to Scutari, was ordered to Varna, after Lord Raglan had (in May) made such preparations for the campaign as he judged best. By referring to Lord Raglan's general orders in May, it will be seen that he had anticipated those evils which were the principal cause of the after sufferings of the troops, viz., the leaving to the discretion of the commissariat, or even of the soldier himself, the supply of proper food.

That a man must be kept alive to fight, and cannot if in hospital be in the trenches, would seem to be a truth, though a truth not recognized in general by military authorities, though certainly Napoleon considered that the principal qualities required to make a great military commander were civil ones. Yet, in a country where the soldier was necessarily dependent upon the commissariat for every kind of supply, it appears to have been in a very short time left, contrary to Lord Raglan's orders, to the sanitary knowledge of a commissary general, whether the soldier was to live on salt meat, rum and biscuit, and on these alone, or not, and to the sanitary knowledge of the soldier himself, whether he were to purchase vegetables or not, and as far as appears no remonstrances or representations were made at the time they ought to have been made, viz., in the summer of 1854, by the head of the [Army] Medical Department, who does not appear to have remembered his sanitary functions.

It perhaps needs explaining that soldiers at the time were not given meals but raw rations, which they had to cook themselves. Decent, cooked, food for the troops would be a key concern for Nightingale from then on.

Nightingale went into Lord Raglan's orders for food, tents, etc., showing that the men suffered from lack of food and blankets from the beginning. The meat was generally bad, so that the men were unable to eat their whole ration, and large quantities were thrown away. 'Yet upon these things depends the health of a man, and in the army, above all other trades, the physical state of the employed is the force of the employer. The health of the men is the main engine of the commander.'

Mistakes were made moving the army from the staging grounds in Bulgaria to the Crimea itself. So many men were dying from cholera in the camp that the army had to be moved, as a 'military necessity'. On arrival in the Crimea, the men were so weak from illness that they were ordered to abandon their kits. A further calamity, the ship with replacements – enormous quantities of great coats, blankets and medical supplies – sank in a storm. The men suffered greatly as cold weather came on.

Figure 3.3 'Neglect of the Orders of May'[7]

At Scutari and in Bulgaria, six hours' drill under a burning sun greatly impaired the health of the troops, but we find, in these same general orders, Lord Raglan's precautions for the health of his army as to length of drills, time of day of drills, fatigue duties, etc.

In general the causes of our suffering in Bulgaria were the unhealthy nature of the ground, want of proper food, of proper clothing, of shelter from the sun, and of medical supplies. All the surgeons are unanimous in saying that even in Bulgaria the food was bad, the tents were bad, the transport bad.

The remedy for the food is to have the ration laid down, to have the bread baked and the meat killed, not by contract, but in the army. Other changes in the commissariat will be suggested. The remedy for bad tents is to have good ones and carriage for them. With regard to all these deficiencies, the questions of importance to solve seem to be: why were Lord Raglan's general orders disregarded? . . .

With regard to the famous move to the Crimea, without pretending for one instant to enter into the military question, it may safely be said that, in a sanitary point of view, it appeared the only salvation for the army, which was so reduced in health that, another month in Varna (so it is thought by many high medical authorities) and nothing would have been left of the British Army but its graves. As it was, the men were so weak that it was found necessary, as is well known, to give an order that they should abandon their kits on landing in the Crimea.

Also, the army could not have advanced towards the Danube, even had it been necessary, for the commissariat had neither transport nor supplies. To retreat upon Constantinople would have fatally injured the *morale* of the army. That the sufferings and mortality of the men were frightfully increased by the expedition to the Crimea is, alas! too true. Could they have been prevented?

Nightingale asked, 'Why was no report of the sufferings of the army made by the principal medical officer?' It was his business to report to the commander the state of health of his army, 'and both what he judges to be necessary to secure that health and to be likely to impair it, as well as to take steps to cure disease'. That measures in the Army Medical Department had to be planned 'beforehand' was 'as obvious as that the artillery or transport must be prepared beforehand'.

She spent some time detailing how medical officers in the field were fearful of reporting problems to headquarters. She quoted a high army officer, 'since civilian judgments' on the army were regarded as having lesser value than those of career army officials. Lord Cardigan described the fears felt by the medical officers as follows: 'I found the supply of medicines very inadequate from the first moment that we landed at Varna. I was constantly spoken to by the surgeons themselves, and also by the brigade major, who said that there was great difficulty from the want of medicine. This was in the month of July 1854, when there was a great deal of sickness'.

A pressing letter was sent to Lord Raglan, requesting that he send for the chief of the Army Medical Department at Varna to report on the poor supplies of medicines and 'medical comforts' to the surgeons. But the surgeons were afraid that they would get into trouble with their superiors. 'In short, it appeared to me that there was a great terror of the head of the [Army] Medical Department'. Lord Hardinge explained that he had had to 'manage' the matter by writing Lord Raglan privately, asking him to send for the head of the Army Medical Department to get the medicines, but not to attach blame to anybody. He thus managed to get the medicines. The doctors even asked him not to make any representations at all, but how could he not let Lord Raglan know 'that they had not got medicines, that there was great unhealthiness in the camp, that the men were dying?'

On the crucial issue of the sewers at the Barrack Hospital, an excerpt shows that reports on defects had gone in as early as 4 August 1854. The 'sanitary superintendent', Dr Anderson, reported to Dr Menzies that 'the privies in the south-west angle of the barrack are in disrepair and contaminating the atmosphere in that part of the building, endangering the health of the troops there'. He explained how pipes burst with filth – a code word for faeces – so that the ground floor was 'covered with filth in consequence', while the main sewer was obstructed. It seems that nothing was done to repair the structural defects. Nor did the director of the Army Medical Department in London, Dr Andrew Smith, follow up on the problem for five months.

Not until 18 January 1855 did Dr Smith write to the principal medical officer at Scutari, stating that he had been informed by officers returning home, 'that the sewerage in and about the hospitals at

Scutari was very defective when the army arrived at Constantinople'. He wanted to be informed if it had since been improved, 'to the extent necessary to ensure, so far as it is concerned, the health of the inmates of the establishment'. In fact the sewers had not been improved, while the number of patients had grown enormously.

Lord Hardinge also had severe comments on the faults at the Scutari hospital. It was under Lord Raglan's command, but the reports given to the commission 'did not give such a true account of the extent of the misfortunes as perhaps ought to have been given'. Lord Raglan 'did not receive, at an early period, sufficient information of the extent of the distress; he did not know that the case was so bad'. Lord Raglan sent Dr Hall to make inquiries, but Hall's report 'was to the effect that everything was in capital order'. Hardinge did not think that Lord Raglan was to be blamed, but Dr Hall was, a point of view Nightingale shared. Moreover, Lord Hardinge 'was not aware that any inquiry had been made into the conduct of Dr Hall for giving that incorrect report'. 'It was Lord Raglan's duty to call Dr Hall to account', which he did not do. Raglan did, however, censure Hall for neglect in the transport of soldiers from the Crimea, in a general order of December 1854. The doctor deemed to be responsible for the neglect was dismissed, whereupon Hall appointed him as principal medical officer at the Barrack Hospital, Scutari.

That Dr Hall was made a KCB (Knight Commander of the Bath) offended Nightingale, who rudely renamed the honour (albeit privately) 'Knight of the Crimean Burial-grounds'. Oddly, her detractors make her disapproval of Hall a fault of character on her part, as if she had no reasons for it.

Asked at the inquiry later as to the commander-in-chief's responsibility for the high death rates, Hardinge pointed out that Raglan was distant from the place, and could not be absent from his post during battle. He was asked if Raglan could have made inquiries in a shorter time, to which Hardinge explained that his suspicions of things having gone wrong 'had been corrected by Dr Hall's report; one hardly sees why he should have sent another person down'. Since Raglan died in 1855, obviously he could not speak for himself.

Sidney Herbert, in his evidence to the royal commission, also stressed the fact that Lord Raglan had sent Dr Hall to inspect the hospitals, and received a 'flourishing account of the state of them'. The commander then 'had reason to believe that all was going on well', especially since Hall's evidence had been based on his own direct observations. 'But I apprehend', added Herbert, 'that people have looked upon the state of things at Scutari with very different eyes. I have received throughout extremely contradictory evidence from Scutari: Officers who were there, even quite at the beginning, wrote and said that they had never seen an army hospital more effective; there have been great improvements of late years in hospitals, especially civil hospitals. I think originally too much was expected. At the same time I am bound to say that I think too little was done, but men who have been accustomed to see hospitals in the field would not be so much shocked at discomforts and deficiencies as civilians would be, who had never seen a hospital established in war'.

Nightingale would continue to be critical of the complacent reports sent by Dr Hall to his superiors. Much of her analysis was to show that the statistics he gave grossly understated the actual mortality. Those who blame Nightingale for the defects at the Barrack Hospital seem to have ignored the fact that its defects had been reported months before her arrival, and not been remedied, and that Hall covered up the problem.

Dr Hall thus reports (20 October 1854) home to Dr Smith, that he has 'much satisfaction in being able to inform him that the whole hospital establishment here (at Scutari) has now been put on a very creditable footing, and that the sick and wounded are all doing as well as could possibly be expected'. 'I am also happy to inform you that, by the strenuous exertions and unceasing labours of first-class staff surgeon Menzies and the medical officers under him, all our difficulties have been in a great measure surmounted, and in a short time, I flatter myself, we shall have a hospital establishment that will bear a comparison with any one of the same magnitude formed under similar disadvantages, or indeed I may almost venture to say, under any circumstances'.[8]

The Duke of Newcastle, the senior War Minister, filled in further details on the misleading information sent up the chain of command: 'So far from ever having received any official information from the doctors or anybody in command of the misery then existing in the hospitals, when inquiries were immediately sent out to them, they were, to a very great extent, if not entirely denied'. The director of the Army Medical Department in London, Dr Smith, expressed 'entire incredulity' as to the truth of the private communications which he, the Duke of Newcastle, had received. He hoped that the negative reports were exaggerated.

Figure 3.4 The Scutari disaster[9]

The Scutari disaster was a separate problem and must be considered by itself. It was the case of thousands of sick removed 300 miles from the causes which had occasioned the sickness and exposed to another class of risks in the buildings into which they were received.

The buildings were spacious and magnificent in external appearance, far more so indeed than any military buildings in Great Britain, and several of them were, apparently, better suited for hospitals than any military hospitals at home. This merely external appearance was, however, fatally deceptive. Underneath these great structures were sewers of the worst possible construction, loaded with filth, mere cesspools, in fact, through which the wind blew sewer air up the pipes of numerous open privies into the corridors and wards where the sick were lying.

The wards had no means of ventilation, the walls required constant lime-washing and the number of sick crowded into the hospitals during the winter of 1854–55 was disproportionately large, especially when the bad sanitary state of the buildings is taken into consideration. The population of the hospitals was increased, not only without any sanitary precautions having been taken, but while the sanitary conditions were becoming daily worse, for the sewers were getting more and more dangerous and the walls more and more saturated with organic matter.

Some slight improvements were made in the beginning of March 1855. But it was not till the 17th March that effectual measures were initiated for removing the causes of disease in the buildings, viz., by the sanitary commission [sent out from England]. By the month of June the improvements were nearly completed, the proportion of sick had fallen off, and the hospitals had become healthy.

This is the whole history of the frightful Scutari calamity. Even from the very beginning of the occupation of these buildings in October 1854, and before the sufferings of the winter had begun, the mortality was very high, although the number of sick was small, indicating the unhealthy state of the buildings even then. Nothing was done to improve them. But fresh shiploads of sick were passed into them. The mortality of course continued to rise. Still nothing was done. Then came the great Crimean catastrophe, and ship after ship arrived with sick in so exhausted a condition that the foul air of these hospitals was almost certain death to them, and accordingly they died, in the month of February 1855, at 415 per cent per annum. So that, in twelve months, at such a rate, the whole sick population of the hospitals would have perished four times. In February two out of every five cases treated died in the hospitals of the Bosphorus, and at Koulali one out of every two. Well may this incredible mortality teach us a terrible lesson!

The reduction in the mortality, after the sanitary works were begun, is most striking, and it falls eventually to less than a sixth part of what it was when the Barrack and General Hospitals were occupied together in October 1854, and to a nineteenth part of what it was in February 1855.

Our general hospitals have been so deplorably mismanaged in all our wars that the question has been raised as to whether it would not be better to do without them altogether. The experience of Scutari proves that general hospitals may become pest houses from neglect, or may be made as healthy as any other buildings.

These are the facts of Scutari hospitals during the first year of our occupation. Nothing in the sanitary recommendations we have been analysing, unless it be some suggestions made when it was too late, would have led us to suppose that there was anything seriously wrong in the hospitals or that their defects had any share in the destruction of the British sick, who have given a name to these buildings in history. . . .

[Quoting from the House of Commons committee report] When the barrack was re-opened as a hospital, no sufficient pains were taken to repair those pipes, or secure a flow of water, and the pipes soon choked up and the liquid faeces, the evacuations from those afflicted with diarrhoea, filled up the pipes, floated up over the floor, and came into the room in which the necessaries were, extended and flowed into the anteroom, and were more than an inch deep when I got there in the morning; men suffering from diarrhoea, who had no slippers at the time and no shoes on as this flood of filth advanced, came less and less near to the necessary, and nearer and nearer to the door, till at last I found them within a yard of the anteroom performing the necessary functions of nature, and in consequence the smell from this place was such that I can use no epithet to describe its horror . . .

[FN:] A farther misery, and the cause of much disease was, in the autumn of 1854, the placing of tubs in those wards farthest from the privies (in the absence of utensils [bedpans]), to hold the excreta of from thirty or fifty patients afflicted with diarrhoea and dysentery; it is easy to imagine the consequence of this frightful nuisance, and it often became Miss Nightingale's duty to see these tubs removed and emptied by a couple of orderlies, who carried one on a pole between them.[10]

None of these picturesque details is reported in the adulatory literature, nor by the second-hand, critical authors. In 'Answers to Written

Questions' Nightingale kept to a discreet and vague 'filth' on the floor. Here we get the frank 'f-word', with the pathetic point that the men had neither shoes nor slippers – nor was soap provided at the time. Nightingale was presumably never in the men's toilets, but she took care, in the 'confidential report', to quote the graphic details from (male) doctors who were. The portrayal of liquid faeces more than an inch thick, on the move, seems to have been beyond the creative capacities of the BBC.

WAR OFFICE REFORM

For decades after the Crimean War, Nightingale worked to ensure the lowest possible mortality rate in war by the provision of good sanitary conditions and adequate medical and nursing services. She joked about her years of 'service' at the War Office, variously describing herself as a long-term inhabitant of it or even as running it. She routinely drew up plans, rules, regulations, lists of supplies, procedures and training requirements. She furnished them to any and all who needed them, and even took the initiative to send them out when no one thought to ask.

The first practical application from the royal commission occurred with Britain's operations in China in 1857. Nightingale was pleased to conclude that the army's new methods reduced the overall mortality of the troops in China to one-tenth of what it had been, and mortality from disease to one in seven.

Nightingale prepared extensively for an expected British expedition in Canada in 1861, arising from the 'Trent Affair' early in the American Civil War. (US forces had boarded a British ship, the *Trent*, and removed two confederate diplomats, who were on a mission seeking British and French recognition of the confederacy.) It seemed that Britain might get involved in hostilities and sent reinforcements to Canada as a precaution. Nightingale was consulted by the War Secretary, Lord de Grey. Her detailed preparation included estimating

5. The 'magnificent' Barrack Hospital, Scutari from the outside, but 'fatally deceptive' within, cesspools loaded with filth, overflowing toilets and sewer air blowing into the overcrowded corridors and wards. Photograph courtesy of Brian Gerrior.

distances to be covered by sleds and the comparative weights and warmth of blankets and buffalo robes. War was, however, averted. The Americans released the confederate envoys, but did not issue the demanded apology.

Nightingale's grandfather, William Smith, had been a leading member of the movement to abolish the slave trade and slavery in the British Empire. Nightingale's sympathies were obviously with the Northern side, the United States Government, in the Civil War. She assisted it with information on the management of the sick and wounded, down to sending copies of the forms that she had developed for the War Office. There is evidence to indicate that her material was extensively used by the Northern army. She would have made it available to both sides, although her collaborator on the matter, Harriet

Martineau, had argued that the southerners were too degraded to profit from their information. It seems that the largest confederate hospital (Chimborazo, for a time the largest hospital in the world), at Richmond, Virginia, was built on the principles Nightingale advocated. As well, the confederate surgeon general issued a book on field cooking citing her as the author, *Directions for Cooking by Troops, in Camp and Hospital, Prepared for the Army of Virginia.*

Little is known on this subject, but it seems that Nightingale felt that her information was not used to full advantage, by either side. Certainly the Civil War is known for its high mortality. References in correspondence a little later, in the Franco-Prussian War, suggest that 'it was the American adaptation of our plans in their war which resulted in a 10 percent death rate instead of 3 percent', and that the Americans could have done much better if they had followed the advice provided more closely.

Nightingale continued to give advice to the British Army during the Anglo-Zulu War (1879) and Egyptian campaigns (in 1882 and 1885), updating and refining the preparation process. By the Boer War at the end of the nineteenth century she was no longer professionally active, although her forms and procedures were still used. Indeed the Army Medical Corps was using her forms well into the twentieth century.

THE GENEVA CONVENTION, THE FRANCO-PRUSSIAN WAR AND MILITARISM

England and France will not be more humane to the enemy's wounded for having signed the Convention and the Convention will not keep semi-barbarous nations, like Russia, from being inhuman.[11]

Nightingale's involvement with the founding and early work of the International Red Cross is complex. Henri Dunant, whose idea it was, credited Nightingale with the inspiration. He was a civilian Swiss who, in 1859, happened to be near the battlefield of Solferino, in northern Italy, just after battle ended. Dunant saw soldiers left to die in agony. On return to Switzerland he urged the establishment of a voluntary agency to assist the wounded. This in time became the International Red Cross. A major ethical advance it achieved was the principle that the sick and wounded in war should be cared for regardless of national affiliation.

In 1864 Nightingale prepared material for Dr Thomas Longmore, who was negotiating on behalf of the British Government, and wrote him: 'I agree with you that it will be quite harmless for our government to sign the Convention, as it now stands. It amounts to nothing more than a declaration that humanity to the wounded is a good thing'.

But she did not believe that it would do much good: 'It is like an opera chorus. And if the principal European characters sing, We never will be cruel more, I am sure if England likes to sing too, I never will be cruel more, I see no objection'. She explained that a convention was like a religious vow: 'People who keep a vow would do the thing *without* the vow. And if people will not do it without the vow, they will not do it *with*'.

In Nightingale's view the whole premise of the Red Cross was faulty for being based on *voluntary* – that is, non-governmental – provision of relief. The danger was that voluntary efforts allowed the belligerents to neglect their responsibilities, and thus cheapened war. Indeed this was confirmed by events only six years later in the Franco-Prussian War. 'The Prussian government makes war cheap by throwing all its duties and responsibilities with regard to its *sick* men overboard, and leaving us and others to pick them up *if we please. If not, not.* It is exactly what we told our own government in 1864 with regard to the Geneva Convention: "Take care that it in no way diminishes the responsibilities of each belligerent government for its own sick and wounded, and for making preparations in time of peace for its sick and wounded in time of war." *We* are *in fact* paying a large quota to the expenses of the Prussians making war.'[12]

One of the complications of the Franco-Prussian War for Nightingale was that her sympathies were pro-French, for reasons that will be obvious in the excerpts. Yet the crown princess of Prussia was Queen Victoria's eldest child, and a supporter of reformed nursing. Technically France was the aggressor, for Napoleon III had declared war. Nightingale gave her best to both sides, was diplomatic in all correspondence with the crown princess and never took sides publicly. Privately she abhorred Prussian militarism and blamed Bismarck for provoking the French declaration of war.[13]

Nightingale kept her personal preferences quiet, but supported France. Britain was not a belligerent in the war, but was involved in the diplomacy at various stages. Nightingale was asked for help from both sides, which she gave, largely through the voluntary National Aid Society, a forerunner of the British Red Cross. She was decorated by both sides at the end of the war.

Most of Nightingale's writing during the war concerns such practical matters as supplies needed, trained personnel and procedures. She personally gave money for the relief of refugees from the siege of Paris and publicly supported fundraising efforts. 'The organization for war is a matter so essential to national existence that, with the smallest flaw in it, nations are overrun and go to destruction. In war everything is exactly adapted for its end, and the end is carried, for exact obedience is rendered. Where the organization of war is deficient, the consequences are so tremendous that there is no need to dwell on the necessity of organization. We see Prussia in possession of France, France prostrate.'[14]

Much as Nightingale sought to set up well-functioning systems to deal with the misery of war, she appreciated the heroism of individuals who rose to the occasion and did what they could. Caroline Werckner, an Englishwoman married to a Prussian, living in Breslau (now Poland) was a stunning example.[15] Werckner went alone night after night to the railway station to give basic aid to French prisoners-of-war en route to detention camps. No organization assisted the prisoners, while a German lady in the local aid society gave things to their German escorts. Mme Werckner took coffee, wine, home-made bandages and what clothing she could get, beginning with her husband's. Nightingale and her cousin Marianne Galton sent her money, and raised some for her from the National Aid Society. Werckner told Nightingale that some prisoners were already dead from exposure. Others declined food and drink and begged 'Let us die'. Some swallowed what she gave them, and expired. There was little left to their uniforms, as they had traded clothing for warm drink or beer. Some had been more than a week on a train, yet were given only bread and water. The cars were open, and rain came in. Some froze to the floors and had to be cut out with hatchets. Some were frostbitten on both feet. Blackened toes dropped off (Nightingale had seen the same in the Crimean War). The worst cases were taken off at Breslau and put in hospital, where the care was abysmal, as Werckner described it to Nightingale.

Mme Werckner was allowed to do this as an Englishwoman, although she was insulted and received threatening letters, for helping 'the enemies of her country'. She obtained admittance to the station 'by private means' (bribes?). Her accounts reinforced Nightingale's understanding of the horrors of war, and that the worst consequences typically occurred after the battle had ended.

MILITARISM AND THE CAUSES OF WAR

The danger of German militarism is not so much the danger
of war, though that is not small, as that danger to its own
institutions, to its own national progress.
Prussia is going to govern the world.
Prussian supremacy . . . the worst military despotism of
the century, the most intolerable and aggravating
expression of it, because the most contrary to all liberty
and progress.[16]

Interspersed among Nightingale's many letters and memoranda of the Franco-Prussian War are observations on the broader issues of militarism, the causes of war and the relative merits of the two sides.

A military dictatorship seemed likely, one which would absorb 'all the better tendencies' of Prussia. It would also Prussianize the 'far nobler, and better' tendencies of non-Prussian institutions. Nightingale joked about 'declaiming against' Gladstone, then Prime Minister of Britain, 'but only imagine Mr Gladstone without a Parliament! . . . Honest and industrious bureaucracy, a high standard of national education, is not enough to make a great nation. Yet that is all that Prussia has'.

Nightingale considered militarism to be harmful to democratic institutions, not only to Germany itself, but Europe more widely. To a colleague she called the end of the Franco-Prussian War, 'this most terrible moment in all history – when neo-German militarism is even more terrible for the future of Europe than the prostrate misery of trampled France'.

Idealism in war was always a theme in Nightingale's writing. She had seen that war drew out great personal courage in men. She had been touched by the daily, uncomplaining sacrifices of ordinary soldiers in the Crimean War. Her writing is laced with respect for their stoicism and loyalty to comrades. Late in life she continued to send memorials to anniversary celebrations of the Crimean battles.

Yet none of Nightingale's admiration for heroism and self-sacrifice led her to think of war as a *good* thing. Rather, the challenge was how to elicit similar altruism in peace. A commemorative letter asked that the soldiers who showed such great virtues in time of war 'show the same virtues in times of home life in peace'. Even during the Crimean War, when her preoccupations were practical, not philosophical, she was questioning. Notably, on her way to Crimea from Scutari she described her 420 convalescent soldiers as 'returning to their regiments to be shot at again'. Recalling that Pastor Fliedner of Kaiserswerth had called her 'a mother in Israel', she sardonically added that 'a mother in the Coldstreams' would be more appropriate.

Organization for peace was as important to Nightingale as that for war, and she sought to ensure that the state cared for the sick, poor, children, criminals, prostitutes and so forth.

> But *are* the consequences less tremendous when the organization of life is deficient? Can there be anything more appalling in the defeats of war ... in the collapses of Wörth, Sedan, Metz [battles in the Franco-Prussian War], than there is in the standing defeat of industry and independence in England, one tenth of whose population are paupers, in the standing defeat of her attempts to reclaim criminals ... in the standing defeat of all her charities and of all her police and of all her Poor Law-ing to reduce pauperism, vice, prostitution, crime one inch, if they do not increase it indeed? Are these not failures worse than Sedan and Paris?[17]

Nightingale was confident that social science research could lead to social betterment. Her vision of public health care, moreover, depended on the skilful use of research to ascertain the causes of evils, towards the application of remedial measures. This same thinking grounded peace advocacy in the twentieth century. Nightingale's vision of possible applications, however, did not go so far as non-violent conflict resolution, a step not to be taken for another generation.

Nightingale's letters late in life show her still concerned about war. In 1888 she commented disparagingly on W. E. Gladstone's support for Balkan uprisings. Referring to the German Emperor (Wilhelm II, who would be 'the kaiser' during World War I) handing Gladstone the 'Montenegrin sword', she added, 'I hate war'. In 1897, to the husband of a cousin, she reported the comments of the retiring American Ambassador to Britain, Thomas F. Bayard: 'You Europeans have not the least idea of what an European war would be now, with your long-range guns carrying six miles, your Maxims and Gatlings, and above all your ironclads, which, on a fine day in peace can sink *by mistake* one of their own fleet'.[17]

Clearly Nightingale did not glamourize war or privilege resources for it as more important than those for civil life. To elicit the same kind of sacrifice in peace as occurred in war was the object. 'Peace hath higher acts of manhood than battle ever knew.' On learning that her physician cousin, Samuel Shore Nightingale, had volunteered for service in Bombay (now Mumbai), then stricken by plague, she said. 'The age of chivalry is come when people *volunteer* not to kill but to cure.'

Nightingale did not write on advocacy for peace or non-violence as a strategy apart from the occasional brief remark such as those above. Yet she had an influence in those areas. She was mentor to Gopal Krishna Gokhale, mentor of Gandhi, who in turn was a significant source for Martin Luther King Jr, in the American civil rights movement of the mid-twentieth century. King himself opposed American aggression in Vietnam, and the civil rights movement generally helped to encourage the non-violent anti-apartheid movement in South Africa. This line of influence all makes more sense when we consider that Nightingale's chief inspiration was Jesus and the cross (to her, Good Friday was the most important day in the world). Gandhi, although not a Christian, was also influenced by the teachings of Jesus, as were such civil rights leaders as Dr King in the United States and Bishop Tutu in South Africa.

4

Health Care, Nursing and Midwifery

NIGHTINGALE'S APPROACH TO HEALTH AND HEALING

Health is not only to be well, but to be able to use
well every power we have.[1]

Nightingale always understood health to be more than the absence of disease. That social conditions, especially housing, were significant determinants of health she knew only too well. A more holistic approach to health and a concern for health promotion, rather than the cure of disease, became fashionable in the late twentieth century and has continued. These were Nightingale's concerns throughout her life and they permeate her writing from official reports on the health of the army to advice to mothers running their households. One of her many criticisms of medical practice in the Crimean War was that 'No provision was made for systematically caring for the soldier's *health*, but only for his sickness. The chief recognized function of the army medical officer was attending men in hospital, but in no way was it considered his duty to render it unnecessary for men to come into hospital at all'.[2]

Nightingale did not have a good opinion of conventional chemical and drug medicine. God or nature cured and the caregiver's role was rather to provide the right conditions for healing. The nurse's role was no less important than the doctor's: 'The physician prescribes for supplying the vital force – but the nurse supplies it'.[3]

Nightingale's *Notes on Nursing: What It Is and What It Is Not*, first published in 1860, was intended for use in the home, not hospitals, and is much more focused on health than sickness. She brought out several further editions, and translations soon began to appear. In 1861 a new edition was published, with a chapter added on infant care, 'Minding baby', and a new title: *Notes on Nursing for the Labouring Classes*.[4]

Notes on Nursing, in all its editions, is still a good source for Nightingale's central philosophy of health and illness: 'All disease, at some period or other of its course, is more or less a reparative process, not necessarily accompanied with suffering: an effort of nature to remedy a process of poisoning or of decay, which has taken place weeks, months, sometimes years beforehand, unnoticed'.[5]

Medicine is not 'the curative process'. Indeed neither medicine nor surgery 'can do anything but remove obstructions; neither can cure; nature alone cures'. Surgery removes the bullet out of the limb, which is an obstruction to cure, but nature heals the wound. So it is with medicine. The function of an organ becomes obstructed; medicine, so far as we know, assists nature to remove the obstruction, but does nothing more. 'Diet, not medicine, ensures health.' Nature's 'restorative processes' are fresh air, light, warmth, quiet, cleanliness and care in diet.

But even with the best preventive measures in place, some illnesses will occur. For these the least intrusive measures should always be tried first. Hospitals were dangerous places, hence Nightingale's emphasis on home visiting. (Doctors then routinely made home visits, and used offices rarely.) 'District nursing' made it possible for people who could not afford a private nurse to get care at home. Convalescent hospitals (preferably in the suburbs or country) should be used as soon as possible. A patient should not stay a day longer in hospital than necessary, said Nightingale. For a child, not an hour longer. Desirably, acute-care hospitals would have convalescent hospitals associated with them, where possible at the seaside.

Good environmental conditions for health, beginning with clean air and water, are stressed throughout Nightingale's writing. A memorandum to the president of the Poor Law Board in 1865 argued that 'the state of the dwellings of the poor, the sanitary or rather unsanitary state of London in general, is not often taken into account in the ill health it produces, for example, consumption, weakness of intellect, rheumatism', not just typhus and cholera. 'Those who come from the worst dwellings are always the most sickly.' Data on the 'social determinants' of health status would become an obvious and routine concern for later health care planners. Nightingale's views mark her as an early exponent.

Medical science was sorely limited at the time Nightingale began nursing. Reliable treatments and effective drugs were few. Doctors' orders often consisted only of what 'stimulants' to use: brandy, port or champagne. In surgery anaesthetics were only coming into use – Nightingale took supplies to the Crimean War. The use of antiseptics in surgery (to which we now turn) had not yet begun.

A popular theory from the time of the Roman Empire was that miasma, or vapours emanating from decaying matter, caused infectious diseases. It was on this theory that Nightingale based her theory of hygiene, which logically led to thorough measures for the elimination of dirt, waste and filth of all kinds, which also, of course, got rid of germs. Germ theory, by contrast, led logically to quarantine as a solution, and this she resisted; good hygiene, rather, was needed. Ultimately Nightingale acceded to the new view, although she continued to stress prevention, through stringent measures for cleanliness.

When Nightingale began her work in the 1850s germ theory was mere speculation. Louis Pasteur's breakthroughs in the 1860s were not on human diseases, but those of winery stocks and silkworms. English surgeon Joseph Lister then began to speculate on the parallels between Pasteur's germs and the causes of infection in surgical wounds. In 1867 he theorized that it was not the oxygen or other gaseous constituent in the air that caused putrefaction, but 'minute organisms suspended in it'. He could identify no specific germ at this point, but referred rather to 'septic' or 'atmospheric' germs, and 'floating particles'. To destroy them he used carbolic acid, then the 'most powerful antiseptic' known.[6]

Germ theory made many converts in the 1870s. German bacteriologist Robert Koch's discovery of anthrax dates from 1877, and his landmark paper, 'The etiology of traumatic infectious diseases', 1879. It is considered to have provided the conclusive proof needed for the theory. Nightingale's conversion to germ theory took place a little later, in 1885.

Her support of miasma theory over germ theory was shared with major 'sanitarians', or health experts, of the time. Her colleagues Drs John Sutherland and William Farr similarly believed that the causes of infectious diseases were generalized miasms, not specific to one disease. Miasms could be minute, too small to be seen by the unaided eye. They were typically associated with smells, but were not the smells themselves – of course getting rid of the smell often got rid of the disease, because it got rid of the causal germs.

The fundamental difference conceptually between the two theories is that germ theory held that each specific bacillus (germ) caused a specific disease, while in miasma theory multiple diseases could arise from the same miasm. Empirically, of course, the same foul water could cause cholera, dysentery or diarrhoea, as we would understand it, because it contained (different) bacilli that caused all those diseases. Swamps infested with mosquitoes could produce both malaria and yellow fever.

Nightingale approved the syllabus of lectures the medical instructor, John Croft, prepared for the Nightingale School in 1873. Many of the lectures were printed, notably 'Disinfectants and antiseptics', which includes a rudimentary explanation of germ theory, suitable for the time.[7] There are specifics on the available antiseptics and their preferred uses. The lecture ended with the warning that these antiseptics were not substitutes for ventilation, fresh air and cleanliness, Nightingale's point precisely.

Nightingale may never have looked into a microscope, but her colleague Dr Sutherland in 1884 purchased a 'beautiful Vienna micro-scope' to see the cholera bacillus, recently demonstrated by Koch, in Calcutta (now Kolkatta), to be the cause of cholera. It seems that Sutherland's relating the importance of this discovery to Nightingale was what finally led her to abandon miasma theory.

Even after coming around to germ theory, however, Nightingale continued to stress best practice over theory. For her time this was sound advice, for the acceptance of germ theory brought with it no advances in treatment. Identification of specific bacilli of course is essential for the development of vaccines. But sturdy measures of cleanliness remained key for disease control, a point recognized by leading germ theorists themselves. Nightingale's methods were excel-lent at prevention, even before she corrected her theory.

Nightingale's advice on practice evolved. While simple cleanliness was stressed in her early *Notes on Nursing* (pre-germ theory), by 1873 the Nightingale School was itself teaching germ theory and antiseptic practice. By the time she wrote the articles on nurse training and nurs-ing for Quain's *Dictionary of Medicine*, in 1878, although not published until 1883, she had detailed advice to give, with precise quantities of the various antiseptics and disinfectants required (excerpts are given later).

By 1891 Nightingale was so convinced of the utility of germ theory that she wanted to use the visibility of germs to stir up people to action in India. She proposed that village lectures be held, with slides to show germs swimming in polluted water. A letter to the public health organization in Pune, which it published the following year, suggests: 'Probably the village school rooms might be utilized for the lectures, which might be made attractive by object lessons, with the magic lan-tern showing the noxious living organisms in foul air and water'.[8] She noted that such preparations, which were shown at an international hygiene congress in Budapest, produced a strong impression.

Back in England Nightingale continued to monitor nursing practices at St Thomas' in the light of evolving theory and available remedies.

In 1895 she noted that the nurses at St Thomas' had to sterilize their scissors and forceps with steam when they went into the wards in the morning. The home sister (or nursing instructor) told her that the 'chatelaine [a cloth key chain] and wallet' were the 'worst of all – millions of microbes can get into them'.

Nightingale asked operating theatre nurses for updates on best aseptic practice. Notes show her pursuing these inquiries as late as 1896 and 1898, with specifics as to what articles should be boiled, what disinfected and with what solutions. A letter Nightingale wrote to Henry Bonham Carter in 1897 joked that the procedures could be briefly stated: boil 'yourself and everything within your reach, including the surgeon'.

THE NIGHTINGALE SYSTEM OF NURSING

A good nurse must be a good woman . . .
The bad woman, the clever nurse, must be an
idiot if she cannot hoodwink the doctor.[9]

When Nightingale set out to reform nursing in the 1850s, the obstacles were enormous. The educational level of women was low (compulsory, free education was only legislated in 1870 in England). Women were not allowed at university, let alone medical school. There were few schools at all for girls, even for those whose families could afford to pay fees. Most of the women who passed for 'educated' did so thanks to governesses at home.

The class system added further complications. Educated women (to the level noted above) belonged to the higher classes where women traditionally did not take jobs outside the home. It was not only that hospitals were rough places, but 'ladies' did not work for pay even in offices or shops. Women who worked, because they had to, were often barely literate.

Many members of the medical profession opposed the introduction

March 5/96

10. SOUTH STREET,
PARK LANE, W

My dear Miss Ekblom
I learn more from you
than you can learn from
me
Do you think you could
be so very kind as to
write down in English
while you are at
Edinburgh or in Scotland
(you will have no time
here) what you had the
goodness to tell me about
Aseptic things.
for instance
White linen Smocks
short sleeves
your never touching
in a dressing or in using
the Catheter anything
else about the Patient
before it
beds
sterilizing
No sterilizing in the
wards
you say truly that we have
gone back to Antiseptics
in the Wards
name of that gauze
you dislike
&c &c &c &c

6. Nightingale letter to Ellen Ekblom, in Public Health Care (6:370).
Courtesy of Kuopio University Archives, Helsinki, Finland.

of trained nurses into hospitals. The women called 'nurses' then were largely untrained cleaners. Only if a doctor informally gave some instruction to a nurse did she get any. There was no system to provide it, no one paid or trained to ensure that it happened. In hospitals nursed by Roman Catholic religious orders the situation was somewhat different. But, since Nightingale was involved only in the regular, Protestant, voluntary hospitals of the United Kingdom, that is a complication that will not be pursued here.

Nightingale was not the first person to try to reform or otherwise improve nursing, but she was the first who sought to make it a paid profession for women. She herself was deeply religious, and she thought that faith was an excellent motivator and help in such onerous work, but the work itself should be paid, not voluntary, and the qualifications based on trained experience, not religious commitment. Priests and pastors should not be in charge (they could and should help, as chaplains).

The unsavoury reputation of nursing when Nightingale began to see nursing as her mission has been well depicted in such fictional characters as Sairey Gamp, in Charles Dickens's *Martin Chuzzlewit*. Mrs Nickleby, a character in his *Nicholas Nickleby*, was at least respectable rather than slovenly, but ridiculous. Non-fictional accounts similarly portrayed 'nurses' as women of doubtful character or servants who could not get places. Medical assistants had to make rounds at night to see that the wine or beer ordered for the patients was not drunk by the nurses, as an 1848 article, 'Hospital nurses as they are and as they ought to be', reported.

Not only theft, but demands for bribes from patients disturbed Nightingale. As she explained: 'How can a dishonest woman attend to her patients? She will take the patients' food and drink, the hospital things, and even if honest as to these, she will – the cardinal sin in all unreformed nursing – exact petty bribes of all sorts from the patients. And those patients who do not and cannot give will be cruelly, sometimes fatally, neglected, children especially. And how can the patients speak?' The nurse 'ought to be the patients' defender and keeper', she said.

The conditions many nurses had to endure were abysmal. At St Bartholomew's Hospital, in 1854, the nurses slept in wooden cages on the landings outside the wards. Decent living and working conditions for nurses, including privacy, would be concerns for Nightingale throughout her working life.

Ten features of the Nightingale method can be identified from an examination of her work – she never set them out in so many words:

1 Nursing is an independent health care profession, with a specific function of patient care, different from medicine and requiring its own distinctive training.

2 Nurses take their medical instructions from qualified doctors, but obedience must be 'intelligent', meaning with discretion, in contrast with the unquestioned obedience required in the military or in a religious order.

3 In a hospital the nursing staff constitutes a separate department, headed by a matron or superintendent, who is responsible to the hospital board, not the medical staff.

4 The nursing hierarchy consists of:
   • matron or lady superintendent
   • assistant matron (in large hospitals, possibly as a training position)
   • ward sister (or charge nurse)
   • head nurse (training completed)
   • assistant nurse (untrained)
   • probationer (in training).

5 Wards are under the charge of a ward sister, who directs the nurses under her and trains the probationers assigned to the ward. There are salary increments commensurate with increased responsibilities as nurses rise through the ranks.

6 Nursing is fundamentally an art which must be learned by guided practice in the hospital ward, in effect an apprenticeship system.

The probationer takes notes on cases and makes daily journal entries, which are monitored. Lectures and assigned readings by medical instructors are supplementary to learning in the wards. Examinations are conducted by medical instructors.

7   Probationers live in a nurses' home, under the direction of the home sister. The home provides meals, shelter, company and training. The home sister organizes classes, teaches some herself and acts as tutor for those given by the medical instructors. She is responsible for the probationers' health and moral welfare. She may organize supplementary classes in reading and writing if needed. She may give Bible classes or see that they are provided.

8   A training school produces a desirable 'esprit de corps'. Nurses who train together work more effectively together than nurses trained at different schools.

9   To introduce trained nursing into an institution without any requires a certain minimum number of nurses. Desirably a team of matron and trained nurses is sent out together. A trained nurse should never be sent out alone to a hospital lacking a core of trained nurses, lest she fall back to its lower standards.

10 Nursing provides a career worthy of lifelong commitment, so that pensions, holiday time and care during illness must be adequately provided for. The work requires maturity, so that probationers must be of adult age before they begin their training: 23 years was the initial requirement at St Thomas'. No fixed retirement age was stipulated, but the physical demands of the job made it unlikely that nurses would stay on much after 60.

Nightingale chose St Thomas' Hospital as the place for her training school largely because its matron, Sarah E. Wardroper, had already succeeded in bringing in improved nursing standards. She had started there as matron in 1853, to be appointed superintendent of the Nightingale School on its opening in 1860. Nightingale was highly involved in the early stages of planning, on regulations, forms and procedures. Then, once the school opened, Mrs Wardroper ran it for the next ten years largely on her own, in consultation with Henry Bonham Carter as secretary of the Nightingale Fund Council. Nightingale was herself more than busy with other work and did not object.

A crisis in Wardroper's management emerged in 1871, however, and Nightingale from then on was more closely involved in directing the school. The resident medical officer had stopped giving classes to the probationers, which Mrs Wardroper neither protested to him about nor informed Nightingale. He also, it was revealed finally to Nightingale, drank on the job and acted offensively to nurses and probationers (what would later be called sexual harassment). Mrs Wardroper's own judgement became erratic. She favoured unworthy probationers and nurses over the more able and dedicated, as it appeared to Nightingale. She instituted a 'spy system', having (junior) probationers report to her on nurses and sisters senior to them. She even told Nightingale about this as if a good thing. It caused much unhappiness and some of the better nurses and probationers quit.

Nightingale's solution was to force the resident medical officer to resign and replace him with a new one. She chose to work around Mrs Wardroper by appointing a person, under her, to provide instruction to the probationers. Mrs Wardroper continued to control entry to the school, dismissals and appointments. Nightingale would have called the new position 'mistress of probationers and undermatron', but Mrs Wardroper objected. The compromise was the unfortunate title 'home sister', which does not reflect the importance of the position. This person ran the 'home', the residence where the probationers lived. She gave classes herself, and tutored pupils taking classes from the doctors. She was in charge of the nurses' library and bought books on behalf of Nightingale to give to nurses. The long serving home sister, Mary S. Crossland, did much to keep in touch with departing probationers, and kept Nightingale informed in turn of their lives and work. From 1873 on Nightingale liaised with both the matron and the home sister on school matters.

Nightingale began in 1872, as a result of the crisis, to meet regularly with probationers and sisters at the hospital. She took copious notes at these meetings and used them later for giving them advice on their careers and writing letters of reference for them. She typically met probationers (possibly never all of them) at the end of their year's training. With some she remained in contact to the end of their lives, or the end of her working life. For some of those who became matrons at other hospitals she became their ongoing mentor. With many there was an understanding of a meeting roughly every year. They were free to contact her more often if a crisis arose. They brought her their problems with difficult staff and pupils, budgets, meal planning, schedules and wrangles with hospital administrators.

Also as a result of the management crisis, Nightingale began to write 'addresses', or lengthy letters to her probationers. They were typically read at the annual meeting at St Thomas' (by Sir Harry Verney or Henry Bonham Carter) and also printed for private circulation. They were clearly started as an attempt to reach out to the dedicated probationers and nurses who felt discouraged by the matron's tactics. They evidently worked, for matrons and former probationers all over the world counted on getting them, thanked Nightingale for sending them, and commented in years when she did not. The addresses had almost no nursing content, but were heavy on the moral challenges. She continued writing them (although not every year) to 1900.

Nightingale's Christian faith is expressed throughout her writing on nursing, and especially so in these 'addresses'. In that of 1874 she said: 'Each night let us come to a knowledge of ourselves before going to rest, as the psalm says, "Commune with your own heart upon your bed, *and be still*." Is it possible that we who live among the sick and dying can be satisfied not to make *friends* with *God* each night?'[10]

A draft Nightingale wrote while preparing her last letter, in 1900, explains: 'Christ, who never wrote down a word of his doctrine as far as we know, but of mercy to the sick and weak in mind and body, miserable and suffering, the idiots and insane, the old in mind and body, Romans apparently knew nothing. That was brought in by Christ. Mercy, care and kindness to the idiot, the leper, the weak in body and mind, is the truest Christianity. The Christian is a nurse. The hospital is a unique fruit of Christianity – hospitals and asylums.'[11]

The addresses stressed strict adherence to preventive measures – rigorous cleanliness. The 1881 one advised: 'Be as careful in the cleansing of the used poultice basin as in your attendance at an antiseptic dressing. Don't care most about what meets the eye and gains attention.'[12]

Many of the matrons who came out of the Nightingale School had difficulties with their boards or administrators at their hospitals. There were inquiries and investigations, even a House of Lords committee on one matron. Nightingale gave advice and moral support. She sent food parcels and flowers with cheering notes, eggs from the country, game, flowers, coffee. She advised desperate matrons not to quit, and assisted with finding the next post when they had to.

Mentoring matrons was tiring work for Nightingale, but doubtless the spread of higher standards of nursing owes much to these years of ongoing contact. Sometimes matrons who were not former probationers asked for her help, too. Eva Marie Lückes, the young matron of the large London Hospital, came to her and continued to for years. (The two worked together also on state registration.)

Mentoring also had its frustrations. An exasperated Nightingale explained to Henry Bonham Carter, 'I got Miss Williams into St Mary's. And she made a fiasco! I thought Miss Masson the person of all others for Oxford. And she made a fiasco! I was earnest in getting Miss Pringle into St Thomas'. And she turned R.C.!!'[13] Describing a particularly vexing nurse to her cousin, Nightingale called her 'an unmitigated nuisance . . . she gives me the cholera – I shall go to live with the king of the Cannibal Islands'.

Nursing was a dangerous occupation in Nightingale's time (and remains so today). Many nurses and probationers fell ill on the job, and some died. The highest possible standards of cleanliness were matters of life and death. Nightingale had often to search out the causes of outbreaks of disease, and seek administrative remedies in better procedures, equipment and training.

Nightingale considered that a night nurse's post was a more responsible one than a day nurse's, and ought to require a year's experience, and pay more. She liked night nursing and had strong views on its importance and difficulties. The dilemma lay in how to train for it, for doctors and senior nurses were scarce at night, and training was typically concentrated in the daytime. Patient abuse historically occurred mainly at night. The adequacy of night superintendence comes up as an issue at many times, even late in Nightingale's working life.

There were periodic incidents of 'finger poisoning', meaning blood poisoning or septicaemia from contact with diseased wounds, at St Thomas' Hospital. An outbreak in 1878 prompted a comprehensive report on the sanitary defects of the hospital, on which Nightingale wrote notes for improvements. Among other things, she wanted directions to be specifically geared to nurses, not surgeons. There should be an examination to ensure that the nurses and probationers understood them. Particulars on finger poisoning were added to the list of printed duties.

In some cases the use of disinfectants would be inadequate. Nightingale was advised, and in turn she gave advice, that burning bandages with discharges was better than using a disinfectant, and the same for bedding: 'fire is the right thing if a thing is so bad that it wants disinfectant'.

In 1896 a Finnish nurse training at St Thomas', Ellen Ekblom, contrasted operating room practices between their two countries. Nightingale passed on her observations to Henry Bonham Carter: 'Why do you observe *aseptic* in your theatres and not *aseptic, but antiseptic* in your wards?'[14] Nightingale suspected, as she told Bonham Carter, that 'much illness is caused among nurses and probationers by the *want of aseptic*'. She asked Ekblom to send them their rules on

aseptic practice, which she had printed for distribution to St Thomas'
nurses. Nightingale wished that she had known about Finnish aseptic
procedures when she wrote the nursing article for Quain's *Dictionary
of Medicine*. Even so, and even in the early version of this article, there
is much on the use of disinfectants – evidently Nightingale would have
made more of the distinction between their aseptic use (preventive)
and antiseptic (killing germs afterwards).

THE INFLUENCE OF NIGHTINGALE
NURSING WORLDWIDE

In some cases institutions sent the Nightingale School selected nurses
for additional training, often not as a regular probationer but a
shorter-term visitor or observer. This occurred especially for nurses
from outside Britain. Nightingale also influenced nursing through
meetings with nurses, doctors, officials or other persons concerned
with reform. They visited and corresponded, and Nightingale gave
them extensive briefings. The Bellevue Hospital, in New York City, and
the Waltham Training School, in Boston, are examples.

Some matrons approached Nightingale directly for guidance and
were invited for a meeting, which sometimes developed into a long-
term mentoring relationship. Matrons found that they could frankly
discuss their problems, and get practical assistance, with a lot of
moral support alongside. Notes from these meetings show heavy ses-
sions and often subsequent correspondence, on staffing, meals and
work assignments. Much of the influence on American nursing came
about in this fashion, much more than through direct training at the
Nightingale School.

For England and Scotland more often Nightingale nurses were sent
as teams (desirably both a matron as leader, and a number of trained
nurses) to implant the new methods. Major examples in England are
Lincoln, Manchester, Addenbrooke's Hospital (Cambridge), Leeds,
and Kent and Canterbury. Undoubtedly the most successful was the

Edinburgh Royal Infirmary, beginning in 1872, which became in effect a second 'Nightingale School', and itself sent out trained matrons and nurses to other hospitals. Teams went out to Sydney, Australia, in 1868, and Montreal, Canada, in 1875. Many hospitals, philanthropists and local notables sought Nightingale nurses, but always the requests were more numerous than the trained staff available to go. Some hospitals would not provide adequate salaries, accommodation and the working conditions Nightingale wanted.

Figure 4.1 shows Nightingale's response to an approach from Belfast, a city which would get many Nightingale matrons and nurses: at the Children's Hospital, the Belfast Lying-in Hospital, and a convalescent home for children. Nightingale also assisted as mentor to the matron of its workhouse infirmary.

It was a city Nightingale herself knew from her travels as a young woman with family friends. She of course said nothing of those impressions, or her views on Irish politics, which were liberal and critical of British policy. (Ireland was then ruled entirely by British, Protestant forces; its established church was the minority Church of Ireland; discrimination against Catholics was harsh. She supported disestablishment of the church and equal rights for Catholics.)

Nightingale described Belfast to her mother when visiting in 1852, for meetings of the British Association for the Advancement of Science, as 'quite pretty', and it seemed 'quite a flourishing place', but, 'the town is quite new, quite Protestant, quite Orange'. An Irish Protestant was 'a kind of anomalous monster'.[15] By comparison, 'Dublin is beautiful as a town', especially Sackville Street (later renamed O'Connell). Nightingale had walked out before breakfast and felt 'something of the same pleasure and excitement I felt the first morning I went out in Rome'. And that was a lot. Further, and all to the detriment of Belfast, 'Dublin is a most beautiful town and such a situation, Belfast all that is dull and uninteresting – it is a cross between Geneva and Manchester – that dull animal, an Irish Presbyterian, infests it, that curious anomaly, quite unlike the Scotch Presbyterian'.[16]

Dublin got large numbers of Nightingale nurses: at the Rotunda Hospital, Dr Steevens' Hospital, Sir Patrick Dun's Hospital, the Royal Hospital for Incurables, the Fever Hospital, City of Dublin Hospital, and the St Lawrence's District Home, a Roman Catholic institution with – a rare exception – a Roman Catholic trained at the Nightingale School at St Thomas'.

The letter excerpted in Figure 4.1 sets out what Nightingale considered to be essential to establish nursing well. Nursing in Belfast could not be run from London, so that it was crucial that it be founded on sound principles. Much attention is paid to moral qualities and the differences to be expected from nurses of different social classes. The realistic cost of doing the job well is stressed. That privacy and decent sleeping arrangements for nurses had to be so vigorously expounded says much of what current practices were.

Figure 4.1 Advice on nursing in Belfast[17]

29 January 1874

My dear Madam [Minnie Otway, County Antrim]

I have so very deep an interest in your Belfast Nurses' Home and Training School that, unwilling as I should feel at any time and at this time doubly so, bowed down as I am with sorrow [her father's recent death] and illness and overwork, I cannot but, as you desire it, do as you wish and put down a few words in answer to your questions, although really all that I have to say are truisms: just as much as 'Put hats on your heads and shoes on your feet'.

1. A good nurse must be a good woman: a sick woman cannot be a healthy nurse. To induce good and respectable good women to come to your institution, to induce them to stay, to keep them in health and above deterioration, either of mind, soul or body, you must give them respectable and healthy accommodation, good food and the moral and physical help necessary to keep women up in hospital life which, after all is said

and done that man can say and do for the best, remains and always will remain a great drain upon woman's life, bodily and moral.

Otherwise women 'will keep themselves up', as within the remembrance of us all they *have* 'kept themselves up' by drink, by pilfering among the patients and by the excitement of immoral behaviour.

To draw a class into the nursing career who are above these things, to keep them above the very temptation to these things, must be the very first object of all who wish to improve hospitals and nursing generally. For no doubt can exist, either that women in hospital life require more helps to keep them straight than in family life or domestic service, or that they receive fewer.

2. From my own experience of nurses' training schools in reformed hospitals, I should say that quite as many candidates present themselves from the highest motives out of the uneducated as out of the educated classes. (To come for the sake of earning a livelihood is not only compatible with, but may be one of the highest motives. For to support destitute relations, to be honourably independent, *is* a high motive in itself.) But the highest motives wear off and life becomes only a hardening routine – if we give no food, or not proper food, to the best qualities of these women, and this of course happens more quickly among the uneducated than the educated, and more surely in hospital life than in any other . . .

3. One of the very first essentials for nurses, and for night nurses if possible even more than for day, is that each should have a sleeping compartment, or room with window and partition up to ceiling, each to herself. And as it is most inconvenient and expensive (if not impossible) to contrive these out of an ordinary dwelling house, it is found to be necessary (and cheaper in the end) to build at once something after the construction of the Liverpool Nurses' Home, Miss Merryweather's, or after that of the 'Nightingale Home', St Thomas' Hospital, London (where I may say by the way, the less ornament there is, the better would it look).

To have the best drainage and sanitary arrangements in these nurses' homes is of course of first-rate importance, and if not well provided for at first, can never be provided afterwards, except at inordinate expense. There must be thorough means of giving fresh air to every corner of the home, good warming arrangements, convenient bathroom and sink and W.C. accommodation on each floor, a roomy dining room and good kitchen arrangements, unless these already exist in the hospital.

If possible a classroom (as this building is meant for a training school and may ultimately supply all Ulster with nurses), a sick room, and hot and cold water laid on each floor. These things are either absolutely necessary to preserve the nurses' health, or they save, if properly provided, such an amount of labour as only persons of experience can estimate.

Shall it be said that thriving, prosperous Belfast, justly celebrated for progress in Ireland, quietly celebrated for its medical schools and science, shall be behind Liverpool and London in securing the essentials of a good nursing school?

4. Would you wish a woman to come to you who does not care for decent privacy? Would your committee wish a woman to nurse their own wives or sons or daughters who had no care for this? Could she be a good nurse? Yet private nursing is an acknowledged part of your institution. Or do you expect a woman to stay, to remain a good woman, or to become a better woman if she wishes for decent privacy and has it not? Is it possible for a woman in the unavoidable drive of hospital life, if she has no corner where she can be alone and read a verse to herself, for one little moment morning to night, not to become quite other than you would wish to have about the sick and the dying? (These are no high flown theories, they are actual experience with poor hardworking moral women, and do you wish to have those who are not?) . . .

5. Then, most reformed hospitals wish to attract the gentler sort of woman – gentlewomen in fact – as an important leaven among the nurses in a training school . . .

And no one will say, although you cannot expect gentlewomen to come and be trained if you do not give them a proper 'home', that they need it more than, or so much as, the uneducated. Quite the reverse. The uneducated, the common run of hospital nurses, need it more than the gentlewoman to keep them from falling into the drinking, light-charactered, light-fingered, altogether untrustworthy, untrained, floating population of hospital nurses of twenty years ago, women who took hospital service because they could get no other. And does anyone really suppose that such women as these will carry out medical orders, if at all, as well as the trained respectable sober solid woman?

6. To sum up: a good nurse must be a good woman, and also a healthy woman. And as a general rule you can't have a good woman unless you place her in the circumstances . . .

7th and lastly. As to patching, repairing, adding to and relaying old out-buildings, I know but one experience on this subject, 'tis also my own: Don't throw good money after bad, build new. If you build, build wisely . . .

Finally I wish the Belfast Nursing Institution 'Godspeed' with all my heart and soul, and would like to see it outstrip all its contemporaries, that they may in their turn outstrip the Belfast, and so a healthy race be kept up for a thousand years and a day, to the great good of all sick people and all active women all over the world.

Five years after giving the above advice to Belfast, Nightingale was approached by a woman in Vienna with a similar request for help. The advice she sent this time overlaps in some respects – a good nurse must be a good woman. But there is now more on nurses abusing patients, notably by demanding bribes, and allusions to doctors' expectations of sexual favours of nurses. Nightingale even hinted that a hospital other than the Vienna General would be better to spearhead the reforms in Vienna, if they were to go ahead.

Again, this was a city Nightingale had visited (in 1850, with family friends), but she did not know it well. Her strong anti-Austrian views emerge in the correspondence, for she continued to identify with her land of birth, Italy, so long oppressed by Austria. The historical context thus is quite different from that in the Belfast letter.

Figure 4.2 Advice on nursing in Vienna[18]

17 March 1879

Dear Madam [Marie von Miller]

The state of things which you so well describe, the evils which you so wisely point out, as regards the system (or no system) of hospital nursing in Vienna we have seen and known elsewhere. Nay, more, it seems to be the normal type of hospital nursing in all countries – the natural, that is, savage formation before civilization comes.

Thirty years ago it was the state of hospital nursing nearly all over the world. This country was (and is in many respects) certainly no exception, before public opinion was directed to the subject of the organization of nursing and the means of producing and training good nurses.

(There was some exception in Paris in hospitals nursed by Augustinian Soeurs [sisters] and Soeurs de Sainte Marthe, mainly as my experience led me to think, because the administration was entirely secular. Thus public opinion was brought in, and the soeurs were entirely under their own female head, thus kindness to patients, and absolute morality and discipline were secured and the medical, and most able staff, and school were the third element. Progress, friendly rivalry leading to improvement and the excellent police of publicity were thus all ensured. The free light and air and criticism, so valuable, of public opinion were thus all let in. I do not dwell on this further because we are not discussing the nursing of 'religieuses' [nuns] save for the excellent lesson here presented.)

2. Nothing can be truer than what you say as to the position taken up as a rule by the medical profession with regard to the subject of nursing – great appreciation of the technical skill of a nurse, when they happen to get a skilful one – utter absence, not only of any knowledge of her moral character, but often of any necessity of moral qualities at all for a good nurse. A good nurse must be a good woman. And how is a good woman to be made and kept?

These two things they do not know and often they do not care to know. The very A B C of a nurse is (A) to be sober and chaste, (B) strictly honest and true, (C) and kind and devoted. For (A) how can a drinking woman attend properly to her patients? Strange things go on when the doctors are not there.

One would think that anyone might see how, of all women, a nurse must be, not only not immoral, but must never allow a free word or look. (B) And how can a dishonest woman attend to her patients? She will take the patients' food and drink, the hospital things, and even if honest as to these, she will – the cardinal sin in all unreformed nursing – exact petty bribes of all sorts from the patients. And those patients who do not and cannot give will be cruelly, sometimes fatally, neglected, children especially. And how can the patients speak?

The nurse, who ought to be the patient's defender and keeper, you have in this case to defend the patient against the nurse. And how can the doctors spend their time thus? They never know of it. They little know how the nurses hoodwink them. The bad woman, the clever nurse, must be an idiot if she cannot hoodwink the doctor. Only a good trained matron over the nurses can, so to speak, defend the doctor who really cares for his patients against [the bad nurse]. And only good trained nurses really carry out the doctors' orders at all times.

(C) Kindness and . . . patience with the patients is a sine qua non in a good nurse, and the merely clever nurse may be wanting in all these things. O, the cruelty which may go on in the best medical-staffed hospital behind the backs of the medical staff. How, indeed can they act as matrons and as head nurses? They are, as you well say, 'too much concentrated upon their scientific objects, and moreover the guidance of men will never suffice for women'. That is so true.

For all Nightingale's insistence that doctors be firmly in charge of patient *treatment*, they should not be allowed to run the hospital itself. 'They are not, and do not pretend to be, administrators', she observed. Even 'leading' physicians and surgeons were the first to admit it, she continued. The great progress made in improving nursing in England was 'due to the fact that in many of our hospitals the management of the hospital is in the hands of civilians'. And, of course, 'a staff of women can only be properly looked after and managed by a woman'.

Everybody agreed that training was needed, Nightingale pointed out, 'but the widest possible and most opposite meanings are attached to it'. At St Bartholomew's Hospital, the probationers were put into the wards after everything had been done in them in the morning, only to leave before the late afternoon's work began. Yet they called this 'training'. 'The regular systematic course of a year, with all its tests, current supervision, examination and records, residence in the hospital under the constant eye of a trained and training matron, a trained mistress of probationers, trained ward sisters (head nurses), with classes and lectures and drilling in these by the mistress of probationers and a well cared for "probationers' home" – this is also called "training".'

However, St Bartholomew's had seen the error of its ways and applied to the Nightingale School for a matron and assistants: 'These have begun work and the experiment is now begun at the right end'.

> As the sense to be attached to training is the foundation, the trained matron is the head of the whole system. The rest is only the hands and the body, what the matron does, what she is there for. In every hospital where the nursing has been organized this has been the mainspring. It has been mainly done by the appointment of a trained and training matron. And in the 'applications' for a 'system' which constantly reach us from abroad and at home, the first thing always is to advise them to obtain a trained matron, to advise what her responsibilities, her duties and powers are to be – including selection, appointment, dismissal, having to discipline and governing, etc., of every nurse, head nurse, probationer, etc., in the hospital – subject of course to the approval of the hospital authorities, to whom the matron is herself responsible.[19]

Again Nightingale pleaded for spiritual and moral help for women in nursing, especially a home in which to foster this support. It was 'impossible, if desirable, and it is undesirable, if possible, to expect the class of women which you want to attract into hospital life, respectable young women of the lower middle class, and practical sensible young women of the middle or upper classes, to come into it to be trained if it is not a home and life into which any good mother would like to place her daughter of whatever class'.

Nightingale's final point concerned the choice between building a new hospital, or starting training in an existing one. 'If the hospital is really wanted, if money enough can be collected to build a good sized hospital, if a strong medical staff can then be obtained – yes, by all means build one.' If not it would be better to win over the leading doctors of an existing hospital, preferably not the Vienna General.

INFLUENCE IN THE UNITED STATES AND CANADA

Nightingale had an enormous influence on the early development of nursing in the United States. She was sometimes approached by reform-minded doctors or philanthropists to send trained nurses to them, or to train prospective matrons at St Thomas' for them. In the case of the Bellevue Hospital, in New York City, she was not able to send nurses when asked in 1872. The Nightingale School was then in crisis, and they had made a major commitment to the Edinburgh Royal Infirmary. Instead Nightingale prepared a detailed letter of advice, which was widely circulated and used.

Florence Lees visited American (and Canadian) hospitals in 1873–74, in effect a fact-finding trip at the request of William Rathbone. Lees sent back detailed reports on conditions and acted as an intermediary, especially for New York. She explained, for example, that while there were nursing schools in the United States in 1873, they were 'unfortunately under male supervision'. The Waltham Training School in Boston was a prime example, which Nightingale would later assist in a variety of ways.

Much of Nightingale's influence was made through her mentoring key American nursing leaders when they were early in their careers. She then made arrangements for them to get some training at St Thomas', usually less than the usual year's probation. She facilitated visits to other institutions, invited them for a talk at her home, and sometimes remained in touch for years afterwards. The influence was significant, clearly, for we have the letters and sometimes the memoirs of these (later) nursing leaders, but it was general inspiration and lofty principles, not the detailed advice Nightingale gave to British matrons.

Linda Richards (the first trained nurse in the United States) is a major example, from her visit to London in 1877. Richards took professional standards to numerous other hospitals where she served as matron: Massachusetts General Hospital, Philadelphia Methodist Episcopal Hospital, New England Hospital for Women and Children, Hartford Hospital, University of Pennsylvania Hospital, Taunton Insane Hospital, Worcester Hospital for the Insane, Michigan Insane Hospital, and others. Richards also founded a training school in Kyoto, Japan, in 1886, learned Japanese, and spent four years there.

Canadian-born Isabel Hampton (later Robb) is another example. Hampton had trained at the Bellevue Hospital, was matron at the Illinois Training School for Nurses, at Cook County Hospital in Chicago, then founded the training school at Johns Hopkins University Hospital, in Baltimore. (Nightingale also advised the architect on the plans for this model hospital.)

Hampton was one of numerous Canadians who went to the United States for training, thanks to the lack of training opportunities in Canada. (Canadian doctors at the time were extremely hostile to trained nurses.) Elisabeth Robinson Scovil was another Canadian in the United States, matron at the hospital in Newport, Black Island. Nightingale met with her over several years and corresponded with her, particularly on the care of children.

The Nightingale School, although without Nightingale's direct involvement, provided an important nursing leader in Louisa Parsons, who founded the nurses' training school at the University of Maryland Hospital, and promoted the Nightingale method in many places.

Parsons also served as assistant matron to Hampton at Johns Hopkins University, and was matron of a war hospital in the Spanish-American War. (She had gained her first war experience in the Egyptian campaign of 1885.)

Nightingale influenced nursing at Boston's Waltham Training School, both through its founder, Dr Alfred Worcester, who approached her for advice in 1895, and the next year by mentoring its superintendent, Charlotte Macleod, another Canadian then nursing in the United States. As well, A. L. Pringle, in effect Nightingale's No. 1 pupil, a former matron both of the Edinburgh Royal Infirmary and St Thomas', served as matron there in 1905–06.

Trained nursing was slow in coming to Canada, thanks to medical opposition, and there were major setbacks. Nightingale sent a team to the Montreal General Hospital in 1875, at its request, but the project turned out badly. The matron was Canadian-born Maria Machin, who was keen to return to her country as a matron, having trained in Dresden and then at St Thomas'. She had had to leave the position of 'home sister' or instructor at the Nightingale Home to do so – a major loss to the school. But the Montreal General never built the nurses' home nor the new hospital promised. Sanitary conditions were bad: one nurse died, as did Machin's doctor fiancé. Machin and all her nurses returned to England in 1878, four of them on a ship that was wrecked on a barren island in the St Lawrence estuary. (They all survived.)

District nursing was started in Canada by Charlotte Macleod, who had visited Nightingale when she was matron at the Waltham Training School in Boston. A new organization, the Victorian Order of Nursing, was created in Canada in honour of the Queen's jubilee. But Canadian doctors opposed it. It took the active promotion of Lady Aberdeen, the governor general's wife, and Dr Worcester, of Boston, who gave patriotic speeches to the Ottawa doctors to help sell the idea. Lord Aberdeen paid Macleod's salary as superintendent for the first two years. Nightingale wrote a public letter of support, met with Lady Aberdeen in London, and gave what moral support she could.

THE EVOLUTION OF NURSING PRACTICE

Nursing is, above all, a progressive calling. Year by year nurses
have to learn new and improved methods, as medicine and
surgery and hygiene improve. Year by year nurses are called
upon to do more and better than they have done.[20]

The two articles Nightingale wrote for Richard Quain's *Dictionary of Medicine* are an excellent source on her evolving views of nurse training (the first article) and nursing practice (the second). They were printed one after the other, in dictionary fashion. A revised edition in 1894 shows Nightingale adding some refinements.

Quain's *Dictionary of Medicine* was directed to doctors, not nurses, so that the articles were geared to telling them what they could expect of a trained nurse. Nightingale also used the opportunity to set out what support, working conditions and time off nurses needed in hospitals. We begin with the key subjects of the application of remedies and observation of patients. These make for neither pleasant nor scintillating reading, although they are less trying than Nightingale at full throttle on sewers, drains and the best way to clean bedpans. They serve to make an essential point about the gradually increased responsibilities assigned to nurses. Given the tendency of some recent academic nurses to disparage the Nightingale School as never having gone beyond 'common sense care' or even 'applied housekeeping', these articles are instructive.

It must be remembered that when the Nightingale School started, in 1860, nurses were entrusted with a very limited range of duties (earlier 'nurses' had been in effect cleaners). Even temperature taking was the responsibility of the medical students (men) and 'dressers' (also men). The poor educational level of the nurses (all women) and probably professional jealousy limited the role allotted to nurses.

Rules 1860: You are expected to become skillful in the dressing of blisters, burns, sores, wounds and in applying fomentations, poultices and minor dressings; in the application of leeches, externally and internally; in the administration of enemas for men and women; in the management of trusses and appliances in uterine complaints; in the best method of friction to the body and extremities; in the management of helpless patients, i.e., moving, changing, personal cleanliness of, feeding, keeping warm (or cool), preventing and dressing bedsores, managing position of; in bandaging, making bandages and rollers, lining of splints, etc., . . . to attend at operations; to cook . . .; to understand ventilation . . . by night as well as by day; you are to be careful that great cleanliness is observed in all the utensils . . . to make strict observation of the sick in the following particulars: the state of secretions, expectoration, pulse, skin, appetite, intelligence, as delirium or stupor, breathing, sleep, state of wounds, eruptions, formation of matter, effect of diet or of stimulants and of medicines; and to learn the management of convalescents.[21]

In 1872, in Nightingale's first 'address' to her nurses, the requirement of taking and recording temperatures was recognized. Rebecca Strong, the first probationer who dared to do this – in the class of 1867 – was reprimanded for her initiative.

By the Quain's *Dictionary of Medicine* article, the need to be able to take and record the patient's temperature was specified 'every quarter of an hour in critical cases'. Many more specifics were added as to observation, especially regarding sleep and the state of wounds. The taking and testing of urine was added. The observation of child cases had to be even more accurate than for adults, for they 'cannot tell what is the matter with them'.

Nurses had to be able to pass a catheter, speculum, syringe wounds and the vagina, give injections and use a galvanic battery. More details were specified on fomentations, poultices and minor dressings.

Instead of merely attending at operations the nurse had 'to prepare patients for and manage them after operations and anesthetics'. In case of haemorrhage, the nurse had to be able to apply 'compression by hand or finger, by extemporary tourniquet and plugging'. There was more detail about bandaging and the making of bandages.

The Quain's article on nursing gave detailed instructions about the use of disinfectants – carbolic is mentioned 18 times, with strengths of solution ranging from 1 in 20 to 1 in 100. Where disinfection would not suffice, burning was required:

> Steeping in boiling water with an antiseptic solution (carbolic acid 1 in 100) is the only safe method of disinfection. All washing of dirty linen and bandages should be done outside of the sick room and, if possible, of the house. In a hospital the laundry should be in a separate building.
>
> *Bandages* with pus on them are always to be burnt at once – to be carried straight to the ward fire, or to a furnace. The best economy is to burn them, but one must make up the fire so that the burning shall not smell. Bandages used for fractures, etc., are the only bandages that may be washed. Soak these with chlorinated soda, a diluted pint, then boil them all night with soft soap, soda and chlorinated soda – a quart bottle for the two. The bandages are then to be rinsed in a tub. The boiler must, of course only be emptied in a closet sink.[22]

With all the details as to antiseptic use, Nightingale yet insisted: 'Absolute cleanliness is the true disinfectant'. 'The nurse must be taught the nature of contagion and infection, and the distinctions between deodorants, disinfectants and antiseptics. Mischief done by students and dressers might have been saved, and valuable lives spared, even among surgeons, if such precautions had been always scrupulously observed by them.' The Quain's article also revisited a favourite Nightingale subject, the management of convalescents: 'a whole department of nursing in itself – and the sooner a convalescent, especially a convalescent child, is removed from hospital to a country "home" the better'.[23]

A section on night nursing, another great Nightingale concern, is the last example to be given here. Nightingale was well aware of how much more difficult it was than day nursing. The nurse had to be able to manage patients on her own, without a doctor or senior nurse close to hand. Drinking and patient abuse mainly happened at night, when there was effectively no supervision.

> Night Nursing. The physician or surgeon requires the night nurse to be as good as the day nurse, or even better – for the most critical times of fever and severe surgical injury often occur at night, or in the very early morning. But quite the same kind of business capacity is not required in the night nurse as in the nurse in day charge of wards. Night nurses, to do their work well, must have at least seven or eight hours in bed, where they can sleep undisturbed by day (even horses in the New York 'Horse Hotel', which work by night, have a separate dormitory to sleep undisturbed by day).
>
> They must have hot meals prepared for them when they come off duty in the morning, and before they go on duty at night, besides breakfast at 1 or 2 a.m. They must have one and a half or two hours' exercise . . .
>
> Holidays. All nurses, especially night nurses, must have holidays, as well as occasional recreation. A month's regular holiday in the year is not too much. Yet more do matrons and superintendents and all women filling nursing offices of great responsibility require an annual holiday, if they are to maintain vigour of body and mind, and not to wear out prematurely.[24]

THE STATE REGISTRATION OF NURSES

The issue of a centralized state registration scheme for nurses emerged in 1888 and became an issue Nightingale fought for some years. Eventually state registration would be achieved, but not until after her death. She was never opposed to registration in principle, but rather to the actual proposal made by the Royal British Nursing Association. Nightingale and her colleagues succeeded in getting it watered down and delayed. Obvious as a state system of registration might seem in today's world, there were good reasons for opposing it at the time. Many shared her view that this would set the profession back, provide no additional protection to the public against unfit nurses and generally fail to address the key challenge: improving the practice of nursing itself. The body proposed to oversee registration was also objectionable to Nightingale for over-representing (men) doctors.

Nursing for Nightingale was an art as well as a science, a calling more than a profession. In a paper, 'Sick-nursing and health-nursing', sent to a women's congress in Chicago, she referred to nursing in all of these terms. Statements she made to the effect that nurses could not be trained should be taken with a grain of salt, for she also insisted on the teaching of a scientific component and frequently gave books on medical science to nurses. Yet Nightingale believed from the core of her being that nursing required gifts and devotion not amenable to testing by examination. She was sceptical that three years of training ensured the making of a good nurse. Nurses were, as she once remarked to a priest friend, Benjamin Jowett, master of Balliol College, 'handmaids of the Lord'.[25] Rural public health nurses were 'health missioners'. Nightingale wondered how an unfit nurse could be removed from the register short of conviction for a crime.

As well, and a point now more sympathetically received, Nightingale understood that nursing practice was still evolving and would always be evolving. Whatever certification might mean after three years of training, it could not guarantee competence years later. She was appalled that registration could be for life and suggested instead that nurses needed certificates from *recent* employers. The need for 'continuous education' would later be met with refresher courses, professional development programmes and other measures of 'lifelong learning'.

MIDWIFERY TRAINING AND MATERNITY CARE[26]

With all their defects, midwifery statistics point to
one truth, namely, that there is a large amount of
preventable mortality in midwifery practice, and that as
a general rule the mortality is far, far greater in lying-in
hospitals than among women lying-in at home.[27]

That good maternity care was an essential public task was obvious to Nightingale, for we all have to be born. Midwifery training was the second project undertaken by the Nightingale Fund, in 1861, with the opening of a maternity ward and training programme at King's College Hospital.

Nightingale's non-medical approach to childbirth should seem familiar to modern feminists: childbirth is a natural occurrence, not a disease. At her time few women in Britain in fact gave birth in hospitals, but the vast number who gave birth at home were attended by a 'midwife' with the scantest of training. The dilemma would be how to ensure care by a skilled, trained person without increasing deaths by bringing childbirth into hospitals and thus contact with the sick.

Maternal mortality in childbirth is, even now with the benefit of hindsight, a complicated issue. Childbirth itself has risks, especially from breech births. In Britain and in Europe death rates of 5 per 1,000 births were standard in Nightingale's time, a figure she quoted from the Registrar-General's report. Maternal deaths from childbirth in industrial countries are now counted per million births.

Deaths included both 'accidents of childbirth', the greater number, and deaths of mothers, up to roughly a month after delivery, from what was most frequently called puerperal fever, from the Latin term for 'around childbirth'. The disease, a type of blood poisoning, was painful, entailing thirst, nausea, stomach pains, disturbed bowel movements, acute fever, cold sweats, coma and bilious vomiting. The victim could die in a day or last several weeks. Many infants also died from the disease, although this did not happen at King's College Hospital and Nightingale did not discuss it.

At the time the midwifery training programme began, virtually nothing was known about the cause of puerperal fever, not identified until 1902 as a form of streptococcus. The greater risk of death was 'accidents' of childbirth, for which better training would seem likely to help. The wards were closed and the training halted six years later on account of an unacceptably high mortality rate from puerperal fever. In the first six years of its operation there were 26 deaths out of 780 women giving birth, or 33.3 per 1,000 woman/births. By contrast the average mortality of women giving birth at home in 1867 was 5.1 per 1,000, Nightingale explained in *Introductory Notes on Lying-in Institutions*. Mortality was higher where medical students were permitted to attend, and she accordingly recommended that medical students not be allowed to observe births, but only midwives and physician/accoucheurs (obstetricians). All midwifery wards connected to general hospitals should be closed at once, she advised (advice not taken).

Introductory Notes on Lying-in Institutions is packed with good advice, arrived at after a careful processing of information. Nightingale herself devised and sent out the questionnaires to obtain comparative mortality data. She also drew on Léon Le Fort's material from many European cities, reported in his book on maternal mortality, *Des maternités: étude sur les maternités et les institutions charitables d'accouchement à domicile dans les principaux états de l'Europe*, 1866. But it seems that she was not aware of the reduction in deaths achieved by Ignacz Semmelweiss in Vienna in 1847–48. There he succeeded in bringing down mortality rates by instituting handwashing, with a disinfectant, for all doctors and medical students entering the medical midwifery ward.

Semmelweiss' conclusions had not been based merely on anecdotal evidence from cases personally attended – the usual substance of papers on the subject – but firm, quantitative data, which Nightingale was fully able to understand. Ironically, she had even visited Vienna in 1850, when Semmelweiss was still there but about to decamp for his native Hungary. He had been humiliated for his insistence on disinfectant handwashing, which implicated doctors and medical students. But Nightingale spent little time in Vienna and loathed it for unrelated reasons (its oppression of Italy). Though she routinely visited hospitals on her European travels, she possibly did not even visit the Vienna General Hospital.

Epidemics or upsurges of maternal deaths occasioned studies of a sort, usually the compilation of case notes, with no material that would lead to any change in procedure. The French midwives Nightingale praised for their full two years' training published on technical aspects of midwifery practice, but not a word on puerperal fever, let alone mortality rates from it. Nightingale's own statistical analysis showed 'a large amount of preventable mortality in midwifery practice' and generally more at maternity hospitals than at home.

Nightingale may have known of the views of the role of doctors in spreading puerperal fever of Sir James Y. Simpson, professor of midwifery at Edinburgh University, for she corresponded with him on a related matter, mortality from limb amputations. Simpson, physician to Queen Victoria and the person who first used chloroform as an anaesthetic in childbirth, published a paper in 1851, 'Some notes on the analogy between puerperal fever and surgical fever', which pointed to the 'fingers of the attendant' as crucial for spreading the disease. Simpson's measures to deal with it were not far off Semmelweiss', developed independently, but without the merit of being based on rigorous data. Simpson even condemned Semmelweiss' work. He later informed Nightingale about Le Fort's book, but never mentioned Semmelweiss'.

Simpson's views on the problems of hospitals were generally similar to Nightingale's. As early as 1848 he urged the abolition of 'medical, surgical and obstetric palaces', to be replaced by lying-in hospitals in separate buildings, constructed of iron, which would be easier to wash. In an 1869 article in *The Lancet*, 'Hospitalism: its effects on the results of surgical operations', he used the term 'hospitalism' in his condemnation of hospital-caused diseases.

It is not clear how early Nightingale became aware of the excessive mortality at the midwifery ward at King's College Hospital. She was distracted by the dispute between the matron and the male overseers of her Anglican order (over which Mary Jones and other sisters soon left). Cartwright noted how 'unusually successful' the ward had been in its first year of operation, in 1862–63 (ninety-three women delivered without fatality). When the programme was closed, in 1867, 792 women had been delivered with twenty-eight fatalities, for a rate of 3.5 per cent, when 4 per cent was 'not uncommon in a lying-in hospital'.

Le Fort's data showed that the Paris maternity institutions routinely had death rates over 10 per cent. In 1864 the Maternité, the institution with the most 'perfect' training of midwives, had a rate of 20 per cent.

Nightingale for the next decades looked for ways to re-establish midwifery nurse training in a safer environment, but never found the right place. She considered workhouse infirmaries, for they typically had lower death rates than regular hospitals. They did not have medical students and did not routinely do post-mortems; decided advantages for avoiding puerperal fever. In contrast with other diseases, puerperal fever was one for which death rates were lower among the poorer, more disadvantaged members of society than the better off.

Introductory Notes on Lying-in Institutions made a solid start on maternal mortality and its prevention, typically with a strong and logical opening:

The first step to be taken in the discussion is to inquire, what is the real normal death rate of lying-in women? And having ascertained this to the extent which existing data may enable us to do, we must compare this death rate with the rates occurring in establishments into which parturition cases are received in numbers. We have then to classify the causes of death, so far as we can from the data, with the view of ascertaining whether any particular cause of death predominates in lying-in institutions and, if so, why so?

And finally, seeing that everybody must be born, that every birth in civilized countries is as a rule attended by somebody, and ought to be by a skilled attendant; since, therefore, the attendance upon lying-in women is the widest practice in the world, and these attendants should be trained, we must decide the great question as to whether a training school for midwifery nurses can be safely conducted in any building receiving a number of parturition cases, or whether such nurses must be only trained at the bedside in the patient's own home, with far more difficulty and far less chance of success.[28]

Nightingale described the difficulties of obtaining appropriate data, for there was then no uniform method of recording cause of death, and no common period for which a death would be counted as due to puerperal fever. Making the most of what could be obtained from the Registrar-General, she concluded that mortality was far higher among women delivering in hospital than at home, and that a large amount of those deaths were preventable. She examined other influences that might have affected the results, namely the mother's age, number of pregnancies, duration of labour, general health status, social class and length of time in hospital, both before and after delivery.

Nightingale was firm on the least medical involvement possible. She would ban medical students entirely from attending births. Giving birth 'is not an illness, and lying-cases are not *sick* cases', she argued. 'It would be well . . . to get rid of the word "hospital" altogether and never use the word in juxtaposition with lying-in women, as lying-in women should never be in juxtaposition with any infirmary cases'.

Midwifery wards in general hospitals should be closed at once. Home deliveries were to be preferred, and where midwifery training was provided, it should be given in small institutions, with conditions as close as possible to those at home. Her introductory chapter concludes:

> If we are to have a training school at all, we must, before all things, make it
> as safe for lying-in women to enter it as to be delivered at home, and having
> made up our minds what is necessary for this purpose, we must pay for it.
> Otherwise we would ensure killing a certain number of mothers for the sake
> of training a certain number of midwives.

The data analysis in *Introductory Notes on Lying-in Institutions* was extensive, but advice had to be kept to general principles; for example:

'The evidence further shows that, in any new plan, infirmary wards must be kept quite detached from lying-in wards. They should be in another part of the ground and should be provided with their own furniture, bedding, utensils, stores, kitchen and attendants. The same arrangement, at least in principle, should be carried out at all existing lying-in establishments, and every case of disease should at once be removed from the lying-in wards to the infirmary and be separately attended there'.

Introductory Notes on Lying-in Institutions was promptly attacked by an anonymous reviewer, presumably a male doctor, in the *British Medical Journal*. Without bothering to summarize the key findings of the 'authoress', the reviewer gave his own views. She was 'a great woman truly, and yet a woman', whose sex could be perceived in her 'free and easy . . . perfunctory' analysis. The 'sublime simplicity' of her 'womanly heart' was responsible for her view that childbirth was not a disease, but an entirely natural condition, so that the high death rate at births attended by doctors needed inquiry. The argument was purely 'sentimental', the reviewer concluded, 'yet ingeniously urged as if it were a logical thunderbolt'.[29]

Nightingale's brief section on lying-in hospitals in *Chambers's Encyclopaedia: A Dictionary of Universal Knowledge*, 1890, permits a late take on her views. Now 19 years after *Introductory Notes on Lying-in Institutions*, she was still warning of the dangers of maternity wards and hospitals. Continuous use of midwifery wards appeared 'to be very dangerous to the patients'. Again she cited the lower mortality rates at workhouse infirmaries compared with maternity and general hospitals, noting that giving birth at home 'is safer then either'. She reviewed the improved measures introduced in Paris, where mortality rates had been the worst in the world. Two better methods had been tried, each with good results: one was of a small ward for each patient, cleaned and limewashed after every delivery; the other had two small delivery wards, each with two or more beds, used alternately. Again cleaning and limewashing were done at short intervals.

Major reductions in maternal mortality were a long time in coming. Improvements were made, but great declines in deaths were not achieved until the development of the sulpha drugs in the 1930s and antibiotics in the 1950s.

DISTRICT NURSING

While the bulk of Nightingale's writing on nursing is directed to hospital nursing, she was no less concerned about patient care at home, not least because hospitals were dangerous places to be avoided. The creation of a district nursing system, to provide care for those who could not afford a private nurse, was an early and ongoing object. It had to take second place chronologically for the simple reason that all nurses, including district nurses, had to be trained in hospitals, for only there would they gain experience of the range of diseases necessary.

Nightingale had to insist time and again that district nursing was about *care*, not handing out money or food. In case of such needs the district nurse had to know to which local agencies to turn, but if she herself became known for hand-outs, nursing would 'fly out the window', as she put it in the letter in Figure 4.3. The district nurse had also to know the local regulatory agencies as well.

> Hospitals are but an intermediate stage of civilization. At present hospitals are the only place where the sick poor can be nursed or, indeed, often the sick rich. But the ultimate object is to nurse all sick at home. Where can the sick poor in general be sick? At home – it is there that the bulk of sick cases are. Where can nurses be trained for them? In hospitals – it is there only that skilled nurses can be trained. All this makes real nursing of the sick at home the most expensive kind of nursing at present. Yet no one would wish to convey the whole sick population into hospital, even were it possible, and even if it did not often break up the poor man's home.[30]

Nightingale for many years worked with William Rathbone and

Florence Lees on the creation of the central district nursing system of London, the Metropolitan and National Nursing Association. On the jubilee of Queen Victoria's reign in 1887, money from a fund raised in her honour was directed to a new agency, the Queen Victoria Jubilee Nursing Institute. Nightingale worked behind the scenes on its terms of reference, to ensure high professional standards.

A succinct statement of the purpose and means of district nursing appears in a letter Nightingale wrote to the Diocese of Durham, excerpted in Figure 4.3.

Figure 4.3 Letter on district nursing[31]

---

2 December 1887

So, though she [the district nurse] has, first and foremost, of course, to nurse the patient, to restore perhaps the breadwinner or the mother, and prevent the breaking up of the home – she has, secondly, to recreate the home – to make it a place which the patients *can* recover in from disease too often caused *in* the home – a place which they *can* be healthy in. These are the triumphs, those the glories of her art.

She has, thirdly, not to give relief – for where the nurse gives relief, nursing flies out of the window – but to know when things are wanted for recovery, to what local agencies and charities to apply for them. She has, fourthly, in sanitary defects which individuals cannot remedy, to know what sanitary authority to call in. And thus to make the home healthy.

Under the first head of nursing proper, she carries out the doctor's orders as trained nursing only can, for she nurses under the doctor, takes notes for him, and reports to the doctor, who has no one but her to report to him.

A humble fellow worker with Providence, the district nurse of high character strives to maintain a man's independence, to make his home less intolerable when wife or children are sick, and *he* will then strive to keep from drink (instead of flying to it, if *relief* is given him) perhaps the very purpose for which sickness was sent . . .

> All this costs money. Yes, but it saves money. Trained district nursing saves expense to the parish, makes it possible to nurse incurable cases at home, which otherwise go into the workhouse infirmary – while tiding cases over a temporary illness and setting them on foot so that they need not go either into hospital or infirmary at all.

By 1895 district nursing had been widely established in Britain, but Nightingale had often to repeat the same basic principles to inquirers. Asked to criticize a manuscript on district nursing, she had still to inform and cajole.

> The first thing a district *nurse* has to do is *to nurse*. It is the nursing, the giving ease and comfort (physical) to the patients which gives her influence. They feel their poor bodies relieved by her. But all the preaching inculcated in this manuscript – the tone of which is excellent – will be of no avail unless she has that entrée to the patients' hearts . . .
>
> The district nurse must always be under a doctor – nothing else will save her from becoming herself a 'quack'. And she must write notes for him, the doctor. (b) She must never give money, but she must know the places where things necessary for the patient can be had.[32]

Nightingale insisted on 'at least one year's training in hospital nursing, two in the district', as preparation. She pleaded for better nutrition, especially milk for children. She closed her advice with a point of life-and-death significance, the strict separation of sick from maternity cases, to ensure that disease from the sick person not be carried to an otherwise healthy birthing mother. The great killer of women post-childbirth, puerperal fever, had yet to be identified under the microscope. Precautions had to be taken even without the nature of the bacteria being known. The district nurse cannot be a midwife:

> But *maternity* nursing is one of her most important duties, and to teach the mother how to feed, how to clothe, how to wash the baby – a duty never,

so far as I know, performed by the trained midwife. The ignorance of the mothers on the score of feeding passes belief. Children among the poor scarcely ever get milk – the value of milk is unknown – the infants' mothers commonly say: 'oh they (the infants) always have what we have ourselves'! To enlighten the mothers on these points is one of the most pressing duties of the district nurse . . .

Caution: the district nurse must not go to the mother in childbed except *before* her other cases. She will probably have to wash the mother herself at first. If she goes again in the evening *after* her other cases, she must disinfect herself first.[33]

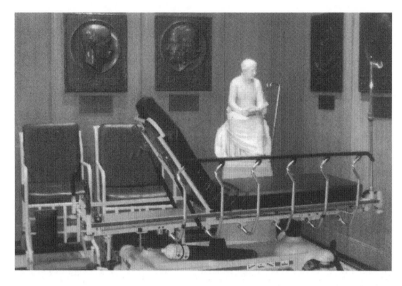

7. Nightingale statue at the Glasgow Royal Infirmary. Photograph courtesy of Sandra Hunter.

5

Workhouse Infirmaries and Hospitals

WORKHOUSE INFIRMARY REFORM

How gladly would I have become the matron of a workhouse.
But, of a visitor's visits, the only result is to break the visitor's
heart. She sees how much could be done and cannot do it.

Years ago, when I visited in one of the great London workhouses,
I felt that visiting had no other effect but to break the visitor's
heart. To nurse efficiently is what is wanted.[1]

From Nightingale's visits to workhouses as a young woman in the 1840s she desperately wanted to bring in fundamental reforms. In time she would go so far as to advocate their effective abolition, by the creation of a welfare system that would give care as needed. Only the 'willfully unemployed' would remain under the harsh conditions of the workhouse.

People were workhouses inmates because they were destitute, but this could be for any number of causes: old age, unemployment, mental deficiency or illness, long-term disability, industrial accident, pregnancy and of course children because of their parents' impoverished condition. There was then no unemployment insurance, workers' compensation, paid maternity leave, old age pension or disability allowance. Nightingale was concerned not only with improving the care of the 'sick poor' in the workhouse infirmaries, but envisioned the virtual abolition of the workhouse system.

The Elizabethan Poor Law was the means instituted for the care of the destitute after the dissolution of convents and monasteries by Henry VIII in the sixteenth century. It gave parishes the duty of providing minimal care for those living within their boundaries. The operative principle was 'less eligibility' – that is, that recipients of assistance should not live better than the poorest self-supporting member of the community. The intention was to dissuade people from seeking relief unless truly desperate. The larger workhouses had their own infirmaries for the care not only of those inmates who fell sick, but the poor in the normal population outside. With no medical insurance (private or public) employed people could exhaust their savings on hospital fees and have to go into a workhouse. There were five patients in workhouse infirmaries for every one in regular fee-paying hospitals.[2]

It is difficult for us today to imagine the horrors of the workhouse infirmaries of Nightingale's time. Material conditions were abysmal: overcrowding, sooty air, shared beds and sleeping on the floor. Toilets and bathing facilities were scarce and nasty. Infectious fever cases were mixed together with other cases. Medical attendance was occasional. There was no provision for drugs, so that the doctor had to pay out of his own stipend for any he prescribed. There was no nursing to speak of; untrained 'pauper nurses', or women inmates not themselves sick, provided what was called 'nursing'. Often these 'nurses' were old and could not lift patients. Few could read. Many drank on the job.

Nightingale had to put workhouse reform on hold for many years from her visits as a young woman. It is clear (in Figure 5.1) that she thought about workhouse nursing during the Crimean War, for a letter to Dr Henry Bence Jones, a physician at her Establishment for Gentlewomen during illness, shows that they continued to discuss possibilities. The letter also is evidence of Nightingale's uncertainty as to how to proceed with this daunting reform after the Crimean War, great as was her desire to help the 'sick poor', those 'who can't help themselves'.

Figure 5.1 Letter on workhouse nursing[3]

Scutari

Barrack Hospital

1 March 1856

The state of the workhouse sick which you describe I am but too well acquainted with, but I have no time at present to make plans, nor to write at length upon any *future* work. By taking the liberty of placing your name upon my council, as I did, I hoped to enlist your advice and support, and to give you the power of 'interfering', as you call it, if I come home, or if I don't. More I cannot predict now.

But one thing I can safely say, if it please God to give me life and health (which seems very doubtful at present), I shall certainly devote that life and health to the one object which we have talked about, and I shall certainly *not* spend any portion of that life in 'training nurses for *rich* families', except *by parentheses*, but shall begin in the poorest and most neglected institution I can find. This is the only plan I have.

I have lost my confidence in government, in boards, in official management of any kind since the awful experience of seventeen months which I have had since I 'joined the army'. But it will be my object to remedy deficiencies among those who can't help themselves, and not among those who can. So that you may safely enlist me for any plan of the kind you mention.

It was only with the generous offer of William Rathbone, a Liverpool philanthropist, that a start could be made. He approached Nightingale in 1864 with the offer to fund additional care in the Liverpool Workhouse Infirmary. His idea, however, amounted to no more than a lady visitor, with comforts to hand out. Nightingale promptly convinced him that no less than trained nursing was needed. The experiment started in May of 1865, with a matron, an idealistic evangelical Christian, Agnes Jones, and a team of nurses from the Nightingale School.

That initial work, against great odds, a difficult workhouse governor (later dismissed), and a whole culture not geared to patient care or women professionals, then was halted with the death, from typhus, of the first matron. Jones could not be effectively replaced: her aunts temporarily filled in, but the next two matrons appointed turned out badly. Later good matrons were found and quality work was re-established, but that was not for some decades.

In the meantime, the opportunity for reform in London itself arose, and Nightingale always believed in the 'bird in hand'. On the death of a Holborn workhouse inmate, from lack of care, Nightingale persuaded C. P. Villiers, the Cabinet Minister responsible for the Poor Law Board, to look critically at the whole system. She explained that the death could have happened in any workhouse infirmary, for skilled nursing was lacking in them all. Villiers responded with enthusiasm, but in fact never got a reform bill drafted, let alone adopted by parliament. He was so overwhelmed with the scope of Nightingale's reforms that he wrote her with a marvellous mixed metaphor, thanking her for the 'peep behind the curtain' she had given him, but 'what the broth will be when it's ready, one can hardly guess'.[4]

In any event Villiers was part of a Liberal government that was replaced in June 1866 by Conservatives with decidedly less interest in social reform. The new Minister, Gathorne Hardy, responded politely to Nightingale's overtures, but gave her only 'half a loaf'. Reforms in workhouse infirmaries would have to be gained one by one. The legislation did not require any actual type or level of reform, let alone care equal in quality to that given in regular hospitals.

Workhouse visitors such as Louisa Twining sought to eliminate abuses in the workhouses – surely a worthy cause – and doctors formed an Association for the Improvement of the London Workhouse Infirmaries, which sought such improvements as better pay for doctors and allowances for prescriptions. But Nightingale's vision (shared with her colleague Dr John Sutherland) was much bolder: that the care given in the workhouse infirmaries should be as good as that in the best-nursed civil hospital in the suburbs. Figure 5.2 gives Nightingale's explanation, to a sympathetic colleague, Edwin Chadwick, of the system-wide reform she was seeking.

Figure 5.2 The ABCs of workhouse reform[5]

---

9 July 1866

The care and government of sick poor and, indeed of all persons labouring under physical or mental disability to win their bread, is a thing totally different from the government of paupers. (Why do we have hospitals in order to cure? and workhouse infirmaries in order *not* to cure? Taken solely from the point of view of preventing pauperism, what a stupidity and an anomaly this is. 'Penny wise and pound foolish', as even a maid-of-all-work could understand.) This is the very first lesson which our legislators have to learn. (But our legislature always mixes up administration with party.)

In order that you may not think me sentimentalizing or politicalizing, I will try to answer your questions one by one:

A. To insist on the great principle of separating the sick, insane, infirm and aged, incurable, imbecile, and above all the children, from the usual pauper population of the metropolis. (How many of those called incurable are *not* incurable a life's hospital experience has taught me. Old age, is, of course, incurable.)

B. To advocate a single central administration.

C. To place all these classes (especially those suffering from any disease, bodily or mental) under this distinct and responsible administration, amenable directly to Parliament.

These are the ABCs of the reform required. Uniformity of system in this matter is absolutely necessary, in order that the suffering poor should be properly cared for, and in order that vacant beds and places may be filled up, wherever space exists. All the officers of these infirmaries and asylums should be appointed by and should be responsible to the central authority, which is responsible to Parliament.

Sickness, madness, imbecility and permanent infirmity are general inflictions affecting the entire community (mainly, too, brought about by the wretched sanitary state of our streets), and are not, like pauperism, to be kept down. The sick or infirm or mad pauper ceases to be a pauper when so afflicted. The past system of mixing up all kinds of poor in workhouses will never be submitted to in future. The very first thing wanted is classification, classification and separation of the lazy, able-bodied, immoral paupers, living on other people's labour, from the sick and infirm.

You must thus have two kinds of administration, one for sick, for infirm, aged and invalids, for insane and imbeciles, and above all for children, and another for paupers. Once acknowledge the principle of this separation and you must have suitable establishments for the care and treatment of sick and infirm.

Nightingale told Chadwick that consolidated administration was essential for efficiency. The guardians might employ nurses rather than pauper nurses (a reform that came in only gradually over decades). They might even appoint lady superintendents, but far more was needed. 'Any attempt' to treat workhouse patients 'as they ought to be treated' would involve more expense than even London could bear, at least in workhouses as they then existed. But there would be economies of scale if 'the entire medical relief of the metropolis' were brought 'under one central management'. The sick could be sent where vacant beds were available, thus using all the establishments 'in the most economical way'. Improvements recently made in army medical services were a positive example. The great Paris hospitals were another example of financial efficiency.

The advantages to medicine and surgery would be 'very great', Nightingale argued: 'We know that, in this way, 6,000 cases of disease and injury would be constantly undergoing examination and comparison in a few large hospitals (which can be built as healthy as the smallest hospitals and far more economically) instead of the experience being fritted away in a few dark dirty rooms here and there, as at present'. A 'thoroughly efficient system of nursing' could be introduced, which was 'impossible' in existing workhouses. A sufficient number of patients was needed, as were probationers, many of whom might come from the workhouse schools.

The practical and the visionary are melded in this manifesto:

Sick, infirm, idiots and mad persons require special constructive arrangements, special medical care and nursing and special dieting. (Of all these, they have little or none that is worthy the name in the present London workhouses.) They are not 'paupers'. They are 'poor and in affliction'. Society certainly owes them, if it owes them anything, every necessary care for recovery. In practice, there should be consolidated and uniform administrative arrangements. Sickness is not *parochial*; it is general and human. For sick you want hospitals as good as the best civil hospitals. You want the best nurses you can find. You want efficient and sufficient medical attendance. You want an energetic and wise administration.[6]

Nightingale apologized to Chadwick for the rambling nature of her long letter. She had had to write it at intervals, much at dawn, because she was driven by (other) business. It was for him alone – or he could show it to John Stuart Mill. We don't know if he did, but Mill in fact supported Nightingale's proposal when Gathorne Hardy brought a bill into parliament in 1867.

The letter excerpted in Figure 5.3 shows Nightingale at her political best, making her pitch to the new, Conservative minister she had never met. She even had letters of introduction prepared to try to smooth the way. Hardy remained cool, not surprisingly as her proposal was far too ambitious even for the Liberals. Nightingale was deeply disappointed with the half measures he brought in.

Figure 5.3 Appeal to a Conservative Cabinet Minister[7]

---

25 July 1866

Private. Sir, I am afraid you will think my writing to you an impertinence in any case. I am not sure that I should much diminish that impertinence by enclosing letters of introduction from 'mutual' friends.

I prefer launching at once into my only real excuse for writing to you on the reform of workhouse infirmaries, which is that I have been in communication with the Poor Law Board for some time past on the subject – besides having had opportunities of discussing it with Mr [C. P.] Villiers personally.

But my immediate reason for assaulting you at such short notice is the reading of Dr Edward Smith's report [*Report on the Metropolitan Workhouse Infirmaries and Sick Wards*]. And I need scarcely say that, if I agreed with its practical proposals, I should probably be the only person who did. He appears to be unacquainted with the centuries of consecutive experience which have led to the adoption of a certain minimum of space for the sick. And he rests his argument for returning to the hospital construction of the Middle Ages on certain experiments of Dr Angus Smith as to the amount of carbonic acid [carbon dioxide] in sick wards, which are not new and which, moreover, have little or nothing to do with the question at issue.

The proposal made by the chief leading medical authorities in London to Mr Villiers, to give 1,000 cubic feet per bed, remains in *no* sense invalidated by Dr Edward Smith's report. Also, Dr E. Smith appears not to have sufficiently considered the fact that, when extensive alterations and additions have to be made to defective buildings, it becomes really more economical to build anew, and *thus* to introduce all the known and established principles of healthy construction into the plans.

Inasfar as regards the nursing and management of sick in workhouses, I speak from a life's experience and say that, if any improvement in this direction is to be carried out, it must be done under a separate organization and management from that of the workhouse. You may perhaps also be aware that, at the Liverpool Workhouse, by the munificence of Mr William Rathbone, an experiment is being tried of introducing trained nurses and training others in the infirmary. We (i.e., the Nightingale Training School) supplied a lady superintendent and twelve head nurses for the purpose. (This has been at work above a year.)

Gathorne Hardy in fact established a committee on cubic space to which Nightingale, late in the day, was invited to submit her views. The request was made 5 January 1867 and she sent in a substantial document on the 19th. By its title it is clear that she went well past its cubic space mandate: 'Suggestions on the subject of providing training and organizing nurses for the sick poor in workhouse infirmaries'. Nightingale was quite good at bootlegging any information she wanted into the topic at hand. In this case she explained up front that the very word 'nursing' had improved its meaning during the last ten years, and was improving every year. She never did deal with cubic space, but stressed the need for adequate *superficial* area, for purposes of nursing efficiency.

The brief acknowledged that the supply of trained nurses available for workhouse infirmaries was poor, and that it did not do to put one trained nurse in an ordinary large workhouse infirmary. She made a concerted case for better training. Sound administrative principles were required, including female control of the nursing staff. Better pay was essential: 'Perhaps I need scarcely add that nurses must be paid the market price for their labour, like any other workers, and that this is yearly rising. Our principle . . . is to train as many women as we can . . . and to find employment for them, making the best bargain for them, not only as to wages, but as to arrangements and facilities for success.'[8]

Nightingale pushed for amendments in Hardy's bill. John Stuart Mill spoke in committee, arguing for Nightingale's point of view on central administration. The Metropolitan Poor Bill was adopted in

1867 and in fact served as the framework from which many reforms in the system were made. Social administration expert Brian Abel-Smith called it 'an important step in English social history ... the first explicit acknowledgment that it was the duty of the state to provide hospitals for the poor', even 'an important step towards the National Health Service Act which followed some eighty years later'.[9]

Since the legislation was permissive only, improvements had to be brought in workhouse by workhouse, which Nightingale, and an increasing number of other concerned persons and organizations, succeeded in doing. The broader 'ABC' of reform she envisaged was not implemented as a system, although many specific improvements were made. The recommendations of the Minority Report of the Poor Law Commission made by Sidney and Beatrice Webb in 1909 can be seen as another step along the way, reflecting this broad vision, now with more detailed consideration of provisions. Even then many recommendations were enacted only partially, to reappear as recommendations in the Beveridge Report at the end of World War II and the postwar establishment of the welfare state in Britain.

The opinion of Nightingale detractors that she abandoned workhouse reform on Agnes Jones's death in 1868 is entirely wrong. There were setbacks, to be sure, notably at the Liverpool Workhouse Infirmary, for which a good replacement could not be found. It was not until the 1880s indeed that it began to get good matrons and was able to establish a successful training school. In the meantime Nightingale nurses were brought into the new St Pancras Workhouse Infirmary, at Highgate, in London, in 1870, again with setbacks. An excellent matron, Elizabeth Vincent, was found for the St Marylebone Workhouse Infirmary in 1884, where a new training school was established. In 1885 the Paddington Workhouse Infirmary obtained a Nightingale School matron, Jane E. Styring, for whom Nightingale was mentor. She also mentored the matron of the Belfast Union (Workhouse) Infirmary, Ella Pirrie (from 1885 on). From the late 1880s the Birmingham Workhouse Infirmary provided good nursing, with a

St Thomas' trained matron, assistant matron and nurses. Workhouse infirmaries in time established their own training schools and sent out nurses not only to other workhouses but to regular hospitals.

SAFER HOSPITALS

It is a rule without any exception, that no patient ought ever to stay a day longer in hospital than is absolutely essential for medical or surgical treatment.[10]

Nightingale's first work on hospitals, in 1858, preceded her famous *Notes on Nursing*, of 1860, for the very good reason that safe hospitals were essential for any reformed nursing to succeed. The quality of the nursing provided (and indeed of the medical care) matters little if the hospital is badly designed, its wards overcrowded and sewers and ventilation defective. The necessary result in such cases is high death rates among patients, nurses, doctors and other staff. First things first.

Nightingale sent a paper, 'Notes on the Sanitary Condition of Hospitals and on Defects in the Construction of Hospital Wards', to the meetings of the British Association for the Promotion of Social Science in 1858. It was fittingly read by Lord Shaftesbury, who had first proposed the sending of a sanitary commission to investigate Crimean War hospitals. Nightingale's paper was published in the association's proceedings, and expanded in an 1859 edition of *Notes on Hospitals*.

In this influential paper Nightingale addressed the difficulty (still the case today) of judging results by hospital when the type of case and length of patient stay differed greatly. She listed the common information hospitals should collect to make comparisons possible. The causes of unnecessarily high death rates she gave as follows:

1   the agglomeration of a large number of sick under the same roof
2   deficiency of space
3   deficiency of ventilation
4   deficiency of light.

These were the 'four radical defects' in hospital construction. She went on to specify precisely what was needed from light and heat to kitchens and laundries.

In 1863 Nightingale brought out her final version of *Notes on Hospitals*, now with a new preface: 'It may seem a strange principle to enunciate, as the very first requirement in a hospital, that it should do the sick no harm. It is quite necessary, nevertheless, to lay down such a principle, because the actual mortality *in* hospitals, especially in those of large crowded cities, is very much higher than any calculation founded on the mortality of the same class of diseases among patients treated *out of* hospital would lead us to expect'.[11]

She pointed out that, since publication of the first edition, 'great advances' had been made in the adoption of 'sound principles' of hospital construction, and even 'already a number of examples of new hospitals realizing all, or nearly all, the conditions required' for successful treatment could be found.

The first cause Nightingale gave for high death rates, 'the agglomeration of a large number of sick under one roof', did not mean overcrowding, or too many for the space provided, but sheer numbers. It was a 'well-established fact' that, other things being equal, sickness and mortality were in ratio to the degree of population density. 'Since this occurred among the healthy, should we not expect it to occur even more among the sick, whose constitutions are even more susceptible?'

She revisited the disasters of the Crimean War hospitals. The Barrack Hospital at Scutari with up to 2,500 men in it, she recalled, was terribly lacking in ventilation and sewerage. The Castle Hospital at Balaclava, by contrast, was small, located on a height, with sea breezes blowing in. The General Hospital at Balaclava was also small and had some of its sick and wounded spread out in well-ventilated huts. Other sick and wounded were placed in tents, again in small numbers. The hospitals, in short, were not at all comparable. The logical Nightingale explained that 'there is a reason, of course, for everything'. In this case it was 'the simple fact' that agglomeration led to dangers of mismanagement and unforeseen events. General administrative defects were 'sure to be accompanied by want of proper ventilation, want of cleanliness and other sanitary defects'. Scutari was the example *par excellence.*

> If anything were wanting in confirmation of this fact, it would be the enormous mortality in the hospitals which contained perhaps the largest number of sick ever at one time under the same roof, viz., those at Scutari. The largest of these too famous hospitals had at one time 2,500 sick and wounded under its roof, and it has happened that, of Scutari patients, two out of every five have died. In the hospital tents of the Crimea, although the sick were almost without shelter, without blankets, without proper food or medicines, the mortality was not above one half what it was at Scutari, but these tents had only a few beds in each. Nor was it even so high as this in the small Balaclava General Hospital, which had part of its sick placed in detached wooden huts. While in the well-ventilated detached huts of the Castle Hospital, on the heights of Balaclava, exposed to the sea breeze, at a subsequent period, the mortality among the wounded did not reach three percent.[12]

The hospitals were not at all comparable.

The sheer size of the Scutari Barrack Hospital is perhaps best understood in comparison with other hospitals, for the two largest London hospitals, St Bartholomew's and Guy's, had 650 and 550 respectively at the time, while St Thomas' had only 200 beds. The overcrowding at Scutari, in short, was appalling. Said Nightingale in *Notes on Hospitals*, 'If overcrowding, or its concomitant bad ventilation, among healthy people generates disease, it does so to a far greater extent among the sick in hospitals'. She showed that the amount of cubic space in civil hospitals varied between 600 and 2,000 cubic feet per bed, but in some military hospitals it was less than 300 cubic feet, so that 'from 700 to 800 was considered a somewhat extravagant allowance'.[13] In other words, the usual army practice of allotting from 600 to 800 cubic feet per bed in hospitals 'was overcrowding'. Yet, for a while at Scutari, not even half this space was given. Such 'great overcrowding' was 'one element in the disastrous result which followed'.

Nightingale would pay attention both to cubic space and superficial space (adequate amounts needed for attending the patient) throughout her professional life.

Considerable attention was paid to mortality rates in *Notes on Hospitals*, a thorny issue for recording practices had then yet to be standardized. Since the hospital's function was to restore the sick to health, 'as speedily as possible', it was necessary to know 'the proportion of sick restored to health, and the average time which has been required for this object'. A hospital which restored all its sick to health with an average of six months' treatment would not be as good as one which did so in six weeks. Hospital statistics were crucial as to:

- proportion of recoveries
- proportion of deaths
- average time in hospital
- the character of the cases
- proportion of different ages among the sick.

Correct hospital statistics were 'an essential element' in hospital administration.[14]

Notes on Hospitals in this third edition also has a note 'On the mortality of hospital nurses'. Nightingale had to point out that the data, from Dr Farr at the Registrar-General's Office, were 'imperfect', and argued that all hospitals should keep a register of nurses. She provided a form to facilitate the tracking of illness and deaths of nurses in hospitals.

Efficiency was another issue for hospitals, the point being to save nurses' energy from lifting and carrying for patient care. This would be a subject to which Nightingale would return repeatedly in criticizing plans for new hospitals or extensions.

She defended the pavilion system as the means to keep hospitals small, in effect each pavilion becoming a mini hospital, with 'as little connection in its ventilation with any other part of the hospital, as if it were really a separate establishment miles away'.

> The essential feature of the pavilion construction is that of breaking up hospitals of any size into a number of separate detached parts, having a common administration, but nothing else in common. And the object sought is that the atmosphere of no one pavilion or ward should diffuse itself to any other pavilion or ward, but should escape into the open air as speedily as possible, while its place is supplied by the purest obtainable air from the outside.[15]

This was written before germ theory had been even partially demonstrated. With the benefit of hindsight, we can see that Nightingale was seeking to minimize the numbers of people breathing the same air and being exposed to each other's germs.

A chapter, 'Improved hospital plans', in *Notes on Hospitals* argued for keeping administrative space entirely separate from patients. A common mistake in hospital construction was to mix together sick wards and administrative offices of all kinds. This led to a complicated structure, different sized rooms, passages and stairs with bad ventilation, 'and diffusing a common atmosphere throughout the building'. Hospital authorities argued that it was cheaper than separating sick and administration, but Nightingale countered that 'such an arrangement exposes both sick and administrators to very unnecessary risks'. It was a cause of fever among administrators, and was 'a danger which should never be incurred on any plea of economy'.

Notes on Hospitals included plans and diagrams of British and French hospitals, good and bad, with explanations as to why. British examples of the bads were (in London) the Royal Free, King's College and the London Hospital; elsewhere, the Royal Victoria Hospital at Netley, the old Manchester Royal Infirmary and the new Glasgow Infirmary. Prominent among the French bads were the Necker (military) Hospital, the old Hôtel-Dieu and Hôpital de La Clinique (a maternity hospital) in Paris.

Good hospitals in Britain were (in London) St Bartholomew's Hospital; elsewhere the Buckinghamshire Infirmary, in Aylesbury, and the new Herbert Hospital, at Woolwich, which last Nightingale said would be 'by far the finest' in the United Kingdom, or indeed in Europe. The good French hospitals were the Lariboisière in Paris, and Vincennes Military Hospital. She also praised three new hospitals in Malta.

A final, general, point: Nightingale considered that non-medical administration was essential for hospitals, for doctors made poor administrators. She joked in an 1859 letter to Sidney Herbert: 'As for doctors, civil and military, there must be something in the smell of the medicines which induces absolute administrative incapacity'.[16]

CHILDREN'S HOSPITALS

On children's hospitals Nightingale began with the basic question as to whether or not to have one. Children's hospitals had become fashionable in her day and continue to be favourite charities. Her instincts were against separate children's hospitals and even separate children's wards, a view reinforced by senior nurses with experience of the several alternatives. Ever the empiricist, Nightingale wanted to know the actual impact on children's lives (with data on mortality, illness and length of hospital stay) as between children's hospitals, children's wards in regular hospitals and mixing children with adult patients.

Nightingale acknowledged the abuse of child patients in hospitals, even where the hospital was nursed by the 'best religious order'. She pointed out that it was a 'tacit idea' among some nuns that it was better for the children 'to die than to live', and that the 'commonest hospital nurses' were sometimes much more tender to the children. Children could not make effective complaints, hence there could be no 'public opinion'. Those who did complain risked nurses taking revenge on them. Also, 'each child may almost be said to require a nurse to itself'.

'Where adults are mixed with them, the woman in the next bed, if the patients are judiciously distributed, often becomes the child's best protector and nurse. And it does her as much good as it does the child. It is a matter of universal hospital experience that this intermingling of ages is essential.'

Nightingale outlined the essentials for children's hospitals, where they were decided upon. There had to be provision for outdoor play and careful separation of bathing facilities. The plan for the Children's Hospital at Lisbon was the 'only plan' to realize 'all the various conditions laid down'. (She had given a detailed critique of it at the request of Prince Albert, although she did not mention that in *Notes on Hospitals*.)

In her article on hospitals for *Chambers's Encyclopaedia*, 1890, Nightingale raised no objection in principle to separate hospitals for children, but argued for facilities for bathing, play (indoors and out), singing and a large garden. Every children's hospital ought to have a convalescent branch at a distance, if possible by the sea. Sick children should never be left alone for a moment, Nightingale stated. If there must be a children's ward in a general hospital, it should be for infants. Again she asserted: 'In all hospitals (in a child's hospital much more than in others) the patient must not stay a day longer than is absolutely necessary'.

Nightingale's article on hospitals for *Chambers's Encyclopaedia* was in fact an update of the entry in earlier editions, which gave a highly favourable account of their merits. The editors kept the opening of the original entry, on the early history of hospitals. Nightingale's wording jumps in with a frank warning of the dangers of hospitals (entirely contradicting the views of the previous author): 'Until the middle of the 19th century the organization and management of hospitals and the nursing of the sick in Britain and in most parts of Europe were, except in some few instances, extremely defective'. That better principles in construction, administration and nursing had been achieved she credited to the arousal of 'public opinion'.

This (1890) publication provides a convenient glimpse of Nightingale's thinking after 30 years of experience (her school at St Thomas' opened in 1860). Her statement on nursing in the 'Hospitals' article is a model of brevity, and a clear expression of her views on health, sickness and the relative roles of nursing and medicine in healing:

Nursing the sick and injured is performed usually by women under scientific heads – physicians and surgeons. Nursing is putting us in the best possible conditions for nature to restore or to preserve health – to prevent or to cure disease or injury. The physician or surgeon prescribes these conditions – the nurse carries them out. Health is not only to be well, but to be able to use well every power we have to use. Sickness or disease is nature's way of getting rid of the effects of conditions which have interfered with health. It is nature's attempt to cure – we have to help her. Partly, perhaps mainly, upon nursing must depend whether nature succeeds or fails in her attempt to cure by sickness. Nursing is therefore to help the patient to live. Nursing is an art, and an art requiring an organized practical and scientific training. For nursing is the skilled servant of medicine, surgery and hygiene.[17]

6

India and Empire

If the facilities for washing were as great as those for drink, our Indian Army would be the cleanest body of men in the world.[1]

Nightingale lived during a period of enormous imperial expansion and consolidation. India came under the direct rule of the British Government, from the East India Company, in 1858; Queen Victoria was proclaimed Empress in 1876. The desirability, or not, of British imperialism seems never to have been a consideration for Nightingale, any more than she considered war in the abstract. The empire was a fact. Government was obliged to serve the common good no less in its colonies and possessions than at home.

What constituted India during the period at issue was quite different from India today. British India was both larger (including parts of what would become Burma, Pakistan and Bangladesh), and smaller (with roughly one-third still under the administration of rajas or maharajahs). The three major components of British India were the 'presidencies' of Calcutta, Bombay and Madras, a term from East India Company days for the headquarters of the presidents of those divisions.

Nightingale began her work on India with optimism about the benefits of British rule. A paper she wrote in 1863, 'How men may live and not die in India', referred to 'one of the most important of social questions', how the British were to hold India, and 'bestow upon' its population the benefits of 'higher civilization'. A paper ten years later, 'Life or death in India', acknowledged that improvements in sanitary conditions had been made, but too few and too slowly. The optimism was gone. There too she attacked the zemindar class, the landowners, for their oppression of the peasants, called ryots.

For Nightingale the India Office and the British civil service in India were lax in implementing recommended reforms. By 1878 she was frankly setting out the failures of British rule. A journal article, 'The people of India', declared bluntly 'we do not care for the people of India'. Instead of providing 'enlightened rule', which should have led to better conditions and lower death rates, Britain took land from the Indians, permitted extortion and usury and let millions die from famine. Numerous articles Nightingale wrote condemned the British administration of India. She increasingly sided with Indian nationals and broke with British officials and experts who failed to take up their cause. She publicly endorsed the parliamentary election campaign of Dadabhai Naoroji, President of the Indian National Congress, who was the first Indian elected to the House of Commons in England.

Nightingale studied Indian society, including its religious practices. She suspected that caste was often used as an excuse 'for not feeding, not cooking for, not cleansing or washing, not housing, not teaching, not amusing, not nursing'. It was necessary to establish how far caste was 'a religious and how far a social institution', how far it could be overcome or how much one must bow to it. A letter recounted that she had been told, 'by an experienced and learned Indian, that we [the English] had made the great mistake of encouraging caste, whereas in India the native idea is that military service does away with caste'.

Nightingale's first involvement with India was prompted by the Sepoy Mutiny of 1857, or the First War of Independence, as Indian nationalists would later call it. She offered to go to nurse the injured soldiers, but her services were not needed and she herself quickly learned that the murders by the Indians were minimal compared with deaths caused by English neglect and mismanagement. 'This massacre killed as many as it is supposed fell by the hands of the mutineers.'

Nightingale's friend Lord Stanley was transferred from the Colonial Office to the India Office in 1858, which gave her the opportunity for action. She lobbied for and succeeded in getting a (second) royal commission appointed, in 1859, with terms of reference on paper confined to the health of the army in India, but quickly broadened to include surrounding communities. An inveterate newspaper clipper, Nightingale added a parable to the clipping from the *Gazette* she kept in her notes:

Parable: The unjust judge and the importunate widow
Dramatis Personae:
Lord Stanley Unjust Judge
F. N. Importunate Widow
Result of 8 months' importunacy [the royal commission].[2]

Sidney Herbert chaired the commission until he was forced to resign from illness, when Lord Stanley took over. The other members included Drs Sutherland, Farr and Alexander, allies from the royal commission on the Crimean War. Nightingale herself devised the questionnaires sent to the Indian stations and analysed the returned data. The final report, a document of over 2,000 pages, was completed in May 1863. She arranged for separate publication of her own 92-page analysis and its circulation to influential people. She lined up sympathetic reviewers for the press and generally managed the media campaign. Her covering letter to Lord Stanley sending the analysed data did not mince words: 'If there be an exception, that is, if there be a single station in India with a good system of drainage, water supply and cleansing for itself and its bazaars [markets], with properly planned and constructed barracks and hospitals, provided with what is necessary for occupation and health – a station where the men are not encouraged to drink, and where they are provided with rational means for employing their time – to such a station these remarks do not apply. But I have not found it'.

Instead, there were 'grievous sanitary defects' everywhere, which could lead only to 'sickness and loss of life . . . cholera, fever, diarrhoea, dysentery and hepatic disease'. She cited Sir Charles Trevelyan,

Governor of Madras, to justify broadening the scope of the report, that 'a good sanitary state of the military force cannot be secured without making similar arrangements for the populations settled in and around the military cantonments, that sanitary reform must be generally introduced into India for the civil as well as the military portion of the community'. Moreover, *now* was the time.

Trevelyan had been a young diplomat in Constantinople when Nightingale arrived to nurse in the Crimean War. She took advantage of their special relationship – he became one of her early collaborators – to urge him to make Madras an example of progress in sanitary reform.

In this report also Nightingale dealt, in print for the first time, with the compulsory treatment of prostitutes for syphilis. 'Lock hospitals and police regulation are, alas! sometimes recommended, just as if they would do any good', she lamented. This would become a major item of *business* from 1863 to 1868, and one she would continue to work on sporadically into the 1890s. She noted that admissions to military hospitals for 'the disease engendered by vice' (syphilis) were five times as great among British soldiers as among the native troops.

The final section of her observations called for the establishment of a sanitary service, for no good would be done, in India any more than at home, 'unless it be made some competent person's express business'. Since there was no local government, this would have to be done by the Government of India. Specifically there was to be a sanitary commission for each of the three presidencies in India, and a sanitary department in the India Office back in London. Nightingale would later see a significant role for local governments in public health, but at this point she still hoped to achieve significant reforms from the top down.

From 1858 on Nightingale devoted a major portion of her time and energy to work on India. This makes good sense for a 'passionate statistician', for India's large population meant that strategic, well-formulated intervention there could save more lives than anywhere else she could work. At that time *millions* still died when there were famines. She published frequently, until late in life, on a wide range of Indian public health and famine prevention issues. She contributed to famine relief herself and helped raise funds from the public. She sent short papers and letters to public health congresses and journals in India. She met with and encouraged Indian nationals who came to London to lobby for various reforms.

Soon after the royal commission on India reported, the then-Viceroy, Lord Elgin, died. Nightingale agitated for his replacement by Sir John Lawrence, a person thoroughly knowledgeable about the country and the need for sanitary reform. His appointment in 1863 provided her with an enlightened and sympathetic person to implement the proposed reforms. Nightingale briefed, cajoled and encouraged the next viceroys as well, until it became a ritual for them to call on her before leaving to assume office.

Nightingale's work towards the introduction of trained nursing in India, however, met with little success, even with the viceroy on side. Lawrence had asked her to draw up a plan for military hospitals, which she did. The government then expanded it beyond recognition (Nightingale always liked to start small to work out any problems). Further, the number of nurses required from England exceeded the numbers available. The Government of India then rejected the plan as too expensive. Trained nursing was brought in, but gradually.

IMPERIALISM, RACISM AND INDEPENDENCE

When Britain assumed full control over India in 1858, a proclamation was issued that provided for the entry of Indian nationals into government positions without regard to race. The practice was quite different. Many years later, in 1883, a bill was introduced in India to extend the admission of Indian nationals to the bench, a measure entirely consistent with the proclamation, although in practice nationals were limited to judgeships in only certain places.

Known as the Ilbert Bill, from its mover, C. P. Ilbert, it was fiercely resisted by Britons in India and their fearful supporters at home. Nightingale joined in the campaign to have it adopted – which it finally was, but in a weakened form.

In the course Nightingale sent a spirited letter to Queen Victoria, asking her to defend her Proclamation of 1858. The Queen did not reply. Nightingale also slipped in some advice on self-government more generally, and the need for government to encourage local industries.

Figure 6.1 Plea to Queen Victoria on India[3]

---

6 August 1883

Private. I again venture with Your Majesty's gracious leave to address the Queen. It is on the subject of the so-called Ilbert Bill, intended to give limited powers to try Europeans, outside of the presidency towns, to native magistrates and judges who, after long trial of their judicial quali- fications in corresponding positions, have shown themselves worthy to be entrusted with this duty, and have risen to that grade where for their offi- cial responsibility such powers are required, that is, to give to a very few trained, tested and experienced native judges, selected by government, the powers to fulfil such responsibilities. It is no mere experiment but has been tried on the bench of the high courts and in the chief magistracies of the presidency towns.

It would be impertinent in me to recall to Your Majesty the gracious Proclamation of 1858, more telling words never announced a nobler sov- ereign mother's will to a more grateful and law-abiding people. It fell like dew upon the thirsty souls of India and it would be unnecessary for me to refer to the Queen's own words that, 'So far as may be, our subjects, of whatever race or creed, be impartially admitted to offices in our service, the duties of which they may be qualified by their education, ability and integrity duly to discharge'. These glorious words have proclaimed that the

Queen will admit the natives of India to share in their own government without distinction of race and creed. The sovereign herself has invited them to educate themselves to qualify for her service, as Englishmen do. In the teeth of difficulty they have, competing with our ablest, obeyed her invitation, and by trial in long service, proved themselves and *not* been found wanting. They know that the Queen's government will not on its side be found wanting . . .

It is stated that there is now scarcely a village among the Queen's 200 millions of subjects in India where it is not known (in the wonderful way in which news flies in Eastern countries) that now is the time when their beloved 'sovereign mother's' proclamation is receiving practical effect, nor where that noble proclamation which 'becomes a monarch better than her crown' is not mentioned *thus* by grateful natives, often with tears of joy and hope.

They refer particularly to the two measures, long promised, now coming at last into more perfect execution of local self-government and of due employment of natives in official positions, together with encouragement of *local industries*.

It is known that a largely signed petition of European ladies of Calcutta and elsewhere in India against the so-called Ilbert Bill, a part, but by no means the most important, of the present just and generous policy, so wisely carrying out Your Majesty's Proclamation, is to be presented to the Queen. May I be permitted to add my deep regrets, to those of many worthier than I, that such a movement should be possible with which the Queen can have no sympathy, and which would find a sufficient answer, were the movers referred to the Queen's own words in that gracious proclamation. Suffer, Madam, me to be the most humble and devoted of Your Majesty's subjects

Florence Nightingale

FAMINE

The aim of my work is to show as well as I can how it is that whole peoples, among the most industrious in the world, on the most fertile soil in the world, are the poorest in the world, how it is that whole peoples, always in a state of semi-starvation, are from time to time on the brink of famine.[4]

Indian famines were mainly occasioned by prolonged droughts and the failure of monsoon rains, but sometimes also by excessive monsoon rains which led to floods. Famines left 'the affected population relatively defenceless against infectious disease'. People died both directly from starvation and by diseases exacerbated by their weakened condition. In the second half of the nineteenth century, the period of British rule in India coinciding with Nightingale's work, an estimated 29 million Indians died of famine.[5] Nightingale herself referred to the estimate of a major famine roughly every 10 or 11 years.

The dominant political philosophy during the British Empire, *laissez-faire* liberalism, meant a rejection of government aid in times of famine. The famine commissioner appointed after the first large famine under full British rule, Sir George Campbell, related in his memoirs that the responsible board 'held by the most rigid rules of the driest political economy, and had the most unwavering faith in the "demand and supply" theory'. They 'rejected almost with horror' the proposal to import grain, so great was their 'zeal for free trade and supply by private effort'. Nightingale campaigned in the opposite direction, arguing for strenuous preventive measures and adequate relief when a famine was under way. She was also aware that resources that could have been spent on famine prevention and relief were diverted to fighting in Afghanistan – and that large numbers of Indians died of famine as a result.

Indian famines prompted the search for causes and remedies, as well as for immediate relief. Nightingale and her collaborators pursued

JOURNAL

OF THE

EAST INDIA ASSOCIATION,

Instituted for the independent and disinterested advocacy and promotion, by all legitimate means, of the public interests and welfare of the Inhabitants of India generally.

THE DUMB SHALL SPEAK, AND THE DEAF SHALL HEAR; OR, THE RYOT, THE ZEMINDAR AND THE GOVERNMENT.

PAPER BY MISS FLORENCE NIGHTINGALE,

READ AT A MEETING OF THE EAST INDIA ASSOCIATION,

ON FRIDAY, JUNE 1, 1883.

THE RIGHT HON. SIR BARTLE FRERE, BART., K.C.B., G.C.S.I.,

IN THE CHAIR.

A LARGE MEETING of the members and friends of the East India Association was held on Friday afternoon, June 1st, 1883, in the Lower Hall, Exeter Hall, Strand, London, W.C., the subject for consideration being "The Land Question in India" as introduced in a paper by Miss Florence Nightingale, entitled "The Dumb shall Speak, and the Deaf shall Hear; or, the Ryot, the Zemindar, and the Government."

The Right Hon. Sir BARTLE FRERE, BART., K.C.B., G.C.S.I., occupied the chair, and amongst those present were the following:— Lord Stanley of Alderley; Sir William Wedderburn, Bart.; Sir George Birdwood, M.D., C.S.I.; Sir James Caird, K.C.B.; Sir George Campbell, K.C.S.I., M.P.; General Sir Arthur Cotton, R.E., K.C.S.I.; Sir Joseph Fayrer, K.C.S.I., M.D.; Sir William Rose Robinson, K.C.S.I.;

No. 3.—VOL. XV.   12

8. Announcement of the reading of a Nightingale paper, critical of British policy, to the East India Association.

a number of interventionist strategies, notably for irrigation. The horror of famine took her away from such issues as nursing and hospitals to those of food production, transportation and government. Her analysis of the social causes of famine in turn prompted her to give greater support for Indian self-government.

Underlying, widespread poverty meant the absence of a buffer against famine. Poverty accordingly became for Nightingale a key issue to investigate. In the course of understanding the causes of chronic poverty, issues of land ownership and taxation had to be pursued, again coming back to self-government. Amartya Sen, the 1998 Nobel laureate in economics, would observe in his *Development as Freedom* that 'no famine has ever taken place in the history of the world in a functioning democracy'.[6] The facts from Nightingale's time are entirely consistent with that point. It is doubtless no coincidence that the early advocates of self-government in India were also leaders in the struggle against famine.

INDIAN WOMEN

Child marriage and 'enforced widowhood' were concerns which engaged Nightingale's sympathies, but issues on which the British Government feared offending conservative Hindu religious sensibilities. Moreover, even some of the most progressive Indian nationals (progressive on other issues) had themselves married as children and saw nothing wrong with it. 'Enforced widowhood' was one consequence of child marriage – that is, the harsh and degrading treatment of a girl who was technically a widow, having been married as a child to an older man, who died before the marriage was consummated. Hindu beliefs then insisted on the isolation and punitive treatment of the girl widow. The British had at least attempted to abolish suttee, or the immolation of a widow on her husband's funeral pyre (although that practice lingered well into the twentieth century). They did not take on child marriage or enforced widowhood.

Dr Mary Scharlieb explained the horrors of this 'death in life' to Nightingale: 'The fact of widowhood is considered to be proof of sinfulness. It matters not whether the wrongdoings that drew down the wrath of heaven were in her present life or in one of her former lives. The crime has been committed, the stain is hers, punishment falls on her in the loss of her lord and master, and for the sake of her eternal welfare, the cleansing fires, actual and material, or potential and spiritual, are her only means of purification, restitution and, *it may be*, of eventual forgiveness'.

Scharlieb described the stripping of the young widow of her clothes and jewels for a rough cloth, head shaving and immersion in cold water; cold rice and water thereafter became her only food and drink.

> Who can wonder at Florence Nightingale's generous sorrow for such sufferings, and who cannot understand her desire to help anyone who was able and willing to give such relief as might be possible to these patient sufferers? Miss Nightingale threw herself enthusiastically into my work; she shared my hopes and fears, and by her great sympathy and powerful interest she helped materially in the completion of the task I had set before me.[7]

The ever-practical Nightingale had a better solution for the lives of widows: offer them training for honourable employment as nurses.

A final point on child marriage, but one for which we have no surviving writing by Nightingale herself, was her behind-the-scenes help to an Indian woman who had been a child bride. The Rukhmabai case became an embarrassment to British authorities, for it showed the untoward consequences of mixing British law, which could be enforced by the courts and jails, with Hindu customary practices, which could not – that is, until British law made those rules enforceable. Rukhmabai was married as a child, but refused to consummate the marriage when of age. The husband took her to court to obtain his rights. Nightingale did a briefing note on the case for the Privy Council, but this document is not available. In time, the husband was paid off and dropped his suit. Rukhmabai was supported actively in her legal case by British Liberal women. She trained as a medical doctor in England and became a leading woman doctor back in India.

The same Dr Scharlieb who had informed Nightingale about child marriage and enforced widowhood was one of the people who persuaded Queen Victoria that Indian women required female medical help – that is, that women would die rather than permit a male medical doctor to examine them. Scharlieb's meeting with the Queen reinforced a plea made earlier by a woman medical missionary, Elizabeth Bielby, to the same effect. The Queen then commissioned Lady Dufferin to see that such services were provided. Lady Dufferin duly formed the National Association for Supplying Female Medical Aid to the Women of India, with Queen Victoria as patron. The association had committees in all the provinces of India. It built hospitals, raising money from Indian philanthropists. The Dufferin Victoria Hospital in Calcutta, for example, treated 20,000 women each year as outpatients, and provided training for women doctors. There were many complications, as hospitals had to make separate provisions for Muslim women, Hindu women, and among the latter, Brahmin ladies.

Nightingale worked with Lady Dufferin not only on female medical aid for Indian women, but also on health education for them in their villages. She went to considerable trouble to find the right sort of health 'primer' needed for rural India. Improvements had to be made locally, Nightingale increasingly came to believe. Women, who managed the household, had to be part of the solution. The situation was complicated as the excerpt in Figure 6.2 shows.

Figure 6.2 Letter on Indian women to Lady Dufferin[8]

---

3 December 1885

I am honoured by your commands to give 'advice and assistance' in your noble scheme for 'reaching' the 'female population' of India, in order to 'teach the most ordinary facts relating to health to the women themselves and to the young girls in schools'. It is indeed a noble scheme, because there is no hope for real sanitary reform – *home* sanitary improvement – till the women are on our side. And I am sure there are some who would work night and day to further your plans. There are of course great difficulties in the way, or rather I should say difficult and special points to be attended to, such as these:

1. At present the highly educated women, e.g., in Bombay, where the women possibly are the best educated, are no better in sanitary arrangements than the poorer.

2. Also the appliances, the habits, the conditions of woman's life, are so different – one might almost say opposite – in Eastern and Western life that one does not know the books or sanitary tracts or booklets which, translated, even if adapted ever so much, would be of use. In fact, they can hardly be adapted.

3. Not only this, but the appliances, the habits, the homes are different in each province – there is a style of house to each province. A sanitary primer for women would have to be written for each province – a native to be looked out (probably a medical man or a clerk to a sanitary commissioner) to write this primer for each province – to be submitted to the sanitary commissioner or to some Anglo-Indian *sanitary* authority *who is conversant* with the *homes*, the domestic family life of the women.

Nightingale's letter went on to the lack of persons able to provide health information. Religious differences meant that

Hindu women are only open to a Hindu woman, Muhammadan women to a Muhammadan woman. None of these to a Christian woman. But this difficulty will be got over by your native lady doctors, if trained and taught in hygiene. The Maratha women are much more open, not bigoted against Christians. And the Parsis are open but quite as insanitary.

Large classes of agricultural women and girls, and even some lower middle-class women, could not read. They could be reached only by 'native lady lecturers', but Nightingale queried if any existed who were instructed 'in hygiene'. The sanitary primer would have to be written in the simplest language, one for each province. She explained:

This is essentially a woman's work. What is desirable (if practicable) is that
Lady Dufferin's native lady medical students should be taught sanitary principles. And then they would be tenfold more useful in giving oral instruction
in patients' houses, or reading and explaining practically to patients' families
the little tracts or primers to be prepared.

Nightingale suggested that it 'might be well to offer prizes to native
ladies for the best essay in home sanitary subjects'.

The caste problem again had to be dealt with:

To teach the ignorant women in the villages, a caste woman must be found,
that is, a Brahmin woman who may teach all castes. A Muhammadan
woman must teach Muhammadan women. These talk Hindustani. The village schools if established must *interest* the girls. And so must these women
sanitary missioners.

As late as 1896 Nightingale was working out a scheme for 'health missioners' for rural India.

OTHER COLONIES

Apart from India, a major subject of her life's work, Nightingale took
on public health issues in other colonies. In 1863 she produced a
report, 'Sanitary state of native colonial schools and hospitals', for the
Colonial Office.[9] She had prepared the forms sent to the governors of
the colonies of Ceylon (Sri Lanka), Australia, Natal (South Africa), the
West Coast of Africa and British North America (Canada).

The Colonial Office at the time was headed by the Duke of Newcastle, who had been the senior War Minister at the beginning of the
Crimean War. Nightingale was, in short, taking advantage of an old
war connection. The Duke was evidently glad to oblige by having the
forms she drew up sent out.

Nightingale's observations are exceptionally strained – she was quite out of her element and the data from different regions were not comparable. But even with such inadequate statistics it was clear that aboriginal people did badly in hospitals and schools. Their mortality rates were roughly twice that of a comparable population not in a residential school or hospital. She strongly recommended careful collection of data to enable authorities to take appropriate measures. But it seems that no action was taken on this advice.

Nightingale in practice gave up the attempt to influence policy through the Colonial Office. She would assist with efforts to improve nursing where asked. But after this first attempt she chose to concentrate on reform in India, where she had allies with whom she could work directly.

High illness and mortality rates of course continued in residential schools, to become in some countries (notably Canada and Australia) issues for apology and compensation in the late twentieth century. Nightingale's mandate included neither cultural genocide nor sexual or physical abuse of children, but only illness and mortality. Yet one is tempted to wonder, if governments had taken her advice to collect data on illness and deaths, and monitored the effects of their administration, if much harm of all kinds might not have been prevented.

7

Nightingale's Legacy

What is the enduring legacy of Nightingale's work, considered a century after her death in 1910? If there had never been a Florence Nightingale, what would we have missed? Are any of her ideas of practical use to us now as we face the challenges of the twenty-first century? What, in effect, did she actually achieve when we examine the record first hand?

Nursing in regular hospitals would doubtless have improved in many respects had Nightingale never been born or given so much of her life to that work. She was not the first and never the only person seeking to improve nursing. Nor was her nursing school the first, or even, in time, the largest. But it was the first training school open to women of any religious affiliation or none at all, and certainly no other school had such an impact on nursing worldwide. Nightingale and her school shaped the early development of nursing not only throughout Britain, but in many parts of Europe (especially in the Protestant German states and Sweden), the United States and the then British Empire, later the Commonwealth, and such major countries as Japan and China.

However much nursing in the regular hospitals might have progressed without Nightingale, it is difficult to imagine any significant advances being made in the workhouse infirmaries, the usual recourse of the 'sick poor'. Other reformers sought to reduce the evils of the workhouse infirmaries, and bring in some comforts, but no one before Nightingale had the vision of raising their standard of care to that of the regular hospitals. Pauper nursing in the workhouse infirmaries was eventually abolished – some 40 years after Nightingale would have done it. High standards of professional care were gradually brought in. She urged the administrative separation of the workhouse infirmaries from the general workhouse system, so that they would not have the stigma of destitution. This was eventually achieved. Nightingale's radical vision of reform also emboldened other reformers to seek more fundamental changes than they had earlier conceived possible.

Nightingale's 'ABCs of workhouse reform' go far beyond the improvement of nursing, significant as that was, to the effective dismantlement of the Poor Law system. If her proposal had been adopted, 90 per cent of the inmates would have been removed from the workhouses, to go to appropriate agencies for their treatment or care, leaving only the wilfully unemployed. New state hospitals and asylums were gradually created: state (general) hospitals, old-age asylums and psychiatric institutions. Nightingale then should be seen as a major contributor to broad social reform in the nineteenth century.

Nightingale has not been given the credit she is arguably due as a social theorist. Sociologists are still prone to see three men only as the founders of their discipline (or, if they recognize more, they too are men). Nightingale, it is said, was not a 'grand theorist' like Karl Marx, Emile Durkheim or Max Weber, i.e., she did not theorize on such lofty subjects as wholesale societal change. But she did! Her conceptualization of a new system of social agencies, with measures for income security, forms the heart of the social democratic reforms of the late nineteenth and twentieth centuries, and the foundation of what was called for some decades in Western countries the 'welfare state'.

The comparison with Marx is particularly instructive. Both were critics of capitalism; both saw its unhappy results in poverty, ignorance and disease. But while Marx considered capitalism to be unreformable, Nightingale believed that it was capable of adaptation. She gave much of her life and work to eradicating the misery it produced by bringing in new, humane measures.

Nightingale saw many reforms achieved in her day, although some of the bolder ones she envisioned did not occur until after World

War II. She had hoped that fundamental changes would be brought in fairly quickly – she was overly optimistic. Rather they had to be struggled for piecemeal. How could a national system of hospital care be realized if 80 per cent of the existing hospitals were still workhouses, nursed by pauper nurses, beds shared and only the most minimal medical care provided, even if other reformers had gotten rid of the rats and improved the food? The National Health Service, launched in 1948, is arguably inconceivable without the changes she worked to introduce from the 1860s.

The reforms Nightingale pressed for at the War Office have been recognized as fundamental and long lasting. Mortality rates in the army, both in peacetime and war, in fact fell when better measures for monitoring disease and treating it were put in place. The pioneering charts she and Dr Farr developed, on preventable mortality rates, were not only taken up by the War Office but extended to data analysis in all areas of social and economic life, from corporate annual reports to environmental assessments.

Nightingale's methodological advice was and remains superb. The studies she herself did were models of new and higher standards of data collection and analysis. The methods she devised became standard practice in mainstream social science. (She used the advice of the Belgian statistician Quetelet for a start, but her own research went well beyond his methodologically.) The term 'evidence-based health care' was not used in her lifetime, but this is what Nightingale was doing. Not a technical statistician, and living before the invention of regression analysis and tests for statistical significance, she nonetheless showed formidable ability to make sense of data and present it persuasively. She has been so recognized by historians of statistics.

It is particularly difficult to assess the lasting legacy of Nightingale's more than 40 years' work on India. She strengthened the progressive forces – the governors and viceroys, other appointed officials and reformers of various kinds on public health, hospitals and nursing, famine prevention, poverty, education and self-government. All this work depended on those in the field, for Nightingale herself never went to India. She remained acutely aware of how the best measures could be undone by complacent officials and opportunists with different political agendas.

Nightingale's role in hospital reform, at the level of design and administration, was also considerable. Neither an architect nor an engineer, she promoted the work of those she thought best saw to health and safety. She criticized plans in their early stages, especially as to their ventilation, choice of materials and site. While so much of her attention went to patient care, she continued to watch over health and occupational safety for nurses, doctors and other hospital staff. Her insistence on design to facilitate nurses' work was also important. Bad design wasted nurses' time and energy, while good design left them more of both for patient care. Again, this influence was worldwide.

Technical innovations have made nearly all of the specifics of Nightingale's advice on hospitals obsolete. Reliance on large wards was needed when nurses had to be able to *see* all their patients. With bells and telephones, and later electronic monitoring devices, that changed. Air conditioning has taken over from ventilation by open windows in industrial countries. Yet one might wonder, with the high and rising number of hospital-caused deaths, if Nightingale's insistence on natural ventilation might be worth reconsidering.

In Canada, with roughly half the population of Britain, and a tenth than that of the United States, an estimated 220,000 people in 2008 fell ill from infections acquired in hospital, and 8,000 died. Nightingale's old-fashioned advice on handwashing has been revived. Perhaps also her advice on natural ventilation should be given a serious trial.

Nightingale's faith is another living legacy, perhaps easier to appreciate now than in her more doctrinaire age. The power of her religious convictions and the years that she lived her commitment as a servant of God, yet a co-worker and friend, too, intrigue. Her respect for other faiths and ability to draw on diverse Christian traditions make her more accessible now than she was in her own time. Much of

Suggestions for Thought would have shocked the devout of her own day – few now, one suspects. Her unmovable 'God of law' might not attract, but who could doubt the passion of her advocacy of a God who was consistently good? Moreover, it is clear that this confidence in a just, benevolent and wise God in fact gave her confidence to pursue her bold reform agenda.

Nightingale's life of faith combined contemplation with intense activity, retreats to refresh and energize, not to escape from the desperate world that needed mending. Her support of missionaries reveals her core evangelical principles. Yet she always respected people of other faiths. Nurses could and should say a word 'in season', to a dying patient, but not harass or proselytize. Their proper job was to nurse, their witness mainly by example.

Nightingale's advice on Afghanistan, as these last words are being written, alas remains germane. She saw and opposed the diversion of revenues for famine prevention and poverty reduction in India (what would later be called 'development') to military incursions in Afghanistan. Britain learned in the course, but later forgot, that Afghanistan was, if easy to conquer, impossible to rule.

Nightingale's legacy to feminism (not a term used then) is more nuanced. She stressed economic opportunities more than political, contrary to the emerging women's organizations of the time. But she contributed her modest bit to the suffrage movement, and to such related issues as property rights and education for women. She led in the opposition to the sexist and degrading 'Contagious Diseases Acts', which targeted women prostitutes to try to reduce syphilis in the army, while ignoring the role of men. Her 'Cassandra', on the limited roles allowed women, was appreciated by later generations of feminists. Her insistence that women have an equal right with men for a life of the mind, to pursue a calling, to live their dreams, must resonate still. John Stuart Mill used her ideas on women in his influential *The Subjection of Women*, 1869.

Nightingale's time predates the emergence of an active peace movement, but her refusal to glorify war, her vivid understanding of the misery of war, and her vision that the real challenge is to extend the self-sacrifice that people will make in war to times of peace, were well ahead of her time. She not only said 'I hate war', but was an example of calling out the best heroism associated with war into making life better in peace on earth.

Endnotes

Notes to A Quick Sketch of Florence Nightingale's Life

1   All the Nightingale material quoted in this book is available, with further background, in a scholarly, peer-review edition, *The Collected Works of Florence Nightingale*, ed. by Lynn McDonald. 16 vols. (Waterloo, ON: Wilfrid Laurier University Press 2001), hereafter referred to by italicized short title and/or volume and page number. Thanks are due the Henry Bonham Carter Will Trust for permission to publish the Nightingale manuscript material, and to librarians and archivists worldwide for assistance in obtaining sources.

2   Stuart Wavell, 'The liability with the lamp', *The Sunday Times* 1 June 2008.

3   F. B. Smith's *Florence Nightingale: Reputation and Power* (London: Croom Helm) was published in 1982; my assessment of it and other material that leaned heavily on it is published in *The Times Literary Supplement* No. 11 (6 December 2000):14–15, which prompted letters-to-the-editor by other scholars adding further instances of his errors. See also Lynn McDonald, 'Appendix B: The Rise and Fall of Florence Nightingale's Reputation', *Life and Family* 1:843–7.

Notes to Chapter 1: The Making of Florence Nightingale

1   Nightingale's letters from Egypt are reported in Gerard Vallee, ed., *Mysticism and Eastern Religions*, vol. 4.

2   Nightingale's recollection of conversion is in a letter of 1895 to Maude Verney, 8:927; Jacob Abbott, *The Corner-stone, or, a Familiar Illustration of the Principles of Christian Truth* (London: T. Ward 1834).

3   'You pray against' from a letter to her sister, 1:317.

4   'I am sorry' letter 20 March 1857, 1:242.

5   On Jowett proposing marriage to Nightingale see Geoffrey Faber, *Jowett: A Portrait with Background* (London: Faber & Faber 1957) 352, and Cornelia Sorabji, *India Calling: The Memories of Cornelia Sorabji* (London: Nisbet 1934) 32; discussed in 1:24–25.

6 'For joy' in 11:318.
7 'active, has a will' 1:26.
8 'disgraceful scenes' in a letter to Sir Harry Verney 3 January 1885, Wellcome Library (Claydon copy) Ms 9010/53.
9 'munificent offer' 1:592–93.
10 Jenny Lind is discussed in 1:550.
11 'fittest homage' 7:100.
12 'perhaps the worthiest' 7:278.
13 On Nightingale's illness see D. A. B. Young, 'Florence Nightingale's fever', *British Medical Journal* 311 (23–30 December 1995):1697–1700; Mark Bostridge, *Florence Nightingale: The Making of a Legend* (London: Farrer, Straus, Giroux 2008) 281–2.
14 'Arctic seas' 1:724.
15 'There is nothing' 1:434.
16 'I never see' 5:819.
17 'Some Scotch doctor' 5:820.
18 'a blessed' 2:562.

Notes to Chapter 2: The Social Reformer

1 Epigraph, 'Essay in Memoriam' 5:60.
2 'These are only' 5:113.
3 'The founder' 5:39.
4 'everything down' from 'A Sub "note of interrogation" what will be our religion in 1999?' 3:29.
5 In *Theology*, 3:12–46.
6 'Darwin' Note, Add Mss 45785 f36.
7 'sin against' 5:653.
8 'I cannot forbear' 5:652.
9 'We should consider' 6:432.
10 'I feel my sympathies' 3:349.
11 'For the rich' 13:260.
12 'none, gentlewoman' 5:103.
13 'it is always cheaper' 5:153.
14 'at least in exceptional' 5:403.
15 'The laws' from 'Politics and public administration' 5:284.
16 'A government' 5:21.
17 Notes on the psalms, 3:553.
18 'A nation' 1:63.

19   'Lord Randolph' 1:373.
20   'is on the Liberal side' 1:63;
21   'working for eternity' 5:653–4.
22   'towards dusk' 4:134.
23   Figure 2.1, Letter to Selma Benedicks, 7:48–50
24   'He had not' 11:432.
25   'Look at' 7:758–59.
26   'the wickedest man' 8:845.
27   'Above all' 3:641.
28   'The pope' 3:94.
29   Figure 2.2, Letter to her family from Rome 7:198–200.
30   'the first man' 7:201.
31   'Cavour' 7:338–39.
32   'most valuable life' 7:330.
33   'Garibaldi's volunteers' 7:553.
34   'coeur d'or' 7:333–34.
35   'Eh bien' note in French, 7:336, also published in *The Times* 11 April 1864.
36   'Whatever influence' 7:338.
37   'Marcus Aurelius' 5:735.
38   'I, like Garibaldi' 7:332.
39   Nightingale's work on the Contagious Diseases Acts is in 8:411–509.
40   Epigraph 1, 11:329.
41   Epigraph 2, 11:114–15.
42   'John Bull' 11:372–3.
43   The debate with St Ignatius, in 11:98.
44   'the Unitarians' 11:96.
45   'Far be it' 11:256.
46   'went about' 11:257.
47   'The God of law' 11:499.
48   Ray Strachey, *'The Cause': A Short History of the Women's Movement in Great Britain* (London: C. Bell 1928) 90.
49   Unpublished in 8:113.
50   Unpublished and printed in 11:422–3.
51   Figure 2.4, 11:591–2.
52   'sublime idea' 11:513.

Notes to Chapter 3: War

1 Epigraph, Evidence of Stafford and MacDonald to a Parliamentary commission; quoted in her Confidential report 130-1, vol. 14.

2 Much of the material is this chapter is from Nightingale's confidential report, *Notes on Matters Affecting the Health, Efficiency and Hospital Administration of the British Army Founded Chiefly on the Experience of the Late War* (London: Harrison 1858), and 'Answers to written questions addressed to Miss Nightingale by the Commissioners', *Report of the Commissioners appointed to Inquire into the Regulations affecting the Sanitary Condition of the Army and the Treatment of the Sick and Wounded* (London: HMSO 1858) 361-94, in vol. 14.

3 See references in 182n 13.

4 'my Pan', Notes ca. 17 November 1856, vol. 14.

5 Figure 3.1, letter, Staatsarchiv zu Berlin Kulturbesitz, vol. 14.

6 Figure 3.2, confidential report preface to Section I, 3-4, vol. 14.

7 Confidential report 6-8, vol. 14.

8 'Dr Hall thus', 'Notes on the sufferings and privations of the Army', confidential report 52, vol. 14.

9 Confidential report, preface, Section III ix and 92, in vol. 14.

10 Figure 3.4, confidential report, preface, Section III ix-x, vol. 14.

11 The epigraph, and all the material on the Geneva Convention, the Franco-Prussian War and other wars are in vol. 15.

12 'The Prussian', letter to Sir H. Verney 1 November 1870, vol. 15.

13 On Nightingale's views of militarism see Lynn McDonald, 'Florence Nightingale and European Wars: From the Crimean to the Franco-Prussian War', *Leidschrift* 22, 2 (September 2007):145-60.

14 'The organization', notes, Add Mss 45843 f203. vol. 15.

15 Correspondence with Caroline Werckner, vol. 15

16 Epigraphs all from notes, Add Mss 45845, vol. 15.

17 'But are', notes 1871, Add Mss 45843 f204, vol. 15.

18 'You Europeans', letter to Vaughan Nash 24 April 1897, University of British Columbia, Woodward Biomedical Library A85, vol. 15.

Notes to Chapter 4: Health Care, Nursing and Midwifery

1 Epigraph, Quain's *Dictionary of Medicine* 1894, 12:735-6. The two major volumes on Nightingale's work on nursing are *The Nightingale School*, vol. 12, and *Extending Nursing*, vol. 13.

2 'No provision', from 'Army sanitary administration and its reform under the late Lord Herbert,' vol. 15.
3 'The physician', Quain's *Dictionary*, 12:715.
4 In *Public Health Care*, 6:17–161.
5 'All disease', *Notes on Nursing*, 12:580.
6 Quotation from Joseph Lister, 'On the antiseptic principle in the practice of surgery', *The Lancet* (21 September 1867):353–6.
7 John Croft, *Notes of Lectures at St Thomas' Hospital* (London: St Thomas/Blades, East & Blades 1873).
8 'Probably the village' 10:363.
9 Epigraphs, 13:475–6.
10 'Each night' 12:804.
11 'Christ, who' 12:880.
12 'Be as careful' 12:851.
13 'I got' 13:192.
14 'Why do you observe' 13:494.
15 'a kind of' 7:711.
16 'Dublin is' 7:713–14.
17 Figure 4.1, Advice on nursing in Belfast, 13:388–91.
18 Figure 4.2, Advice on nursing in Vienna, 13:474–9.
19 'As the sense' 13:478.
20 Epigraphs from Quain's *Dictionary*, 1894, 12:749.
21 'Rules 1860' 12:899.
22 'Steeping in', Quain's *Dictionary*, 12:742.
23 'Absolute cleanliness', Quain's *Dictionary*, 12:742.
24 'Night nursing', Quain's *Dictionary*, 12:749–50.
25 'handmaids' 3:330.
26 All the material on midwifery is in *Women*, vol. 8.
27 Epigraph, *Introductory Notes on Lying-in Institutions*, 8:254.
28 'The first step', *Introductory Notes on Lying-in Institutions*, 8:253.
29 'authoress', from the *British Medical Journal* 28 October 1871, 8:332.
30 'Hospitals are', 'Training Nurses for the Sick Poor', *The Times* 14 April 1876, 13:755.
31 Figure 4.3, Letter to the Diocese of Durham, 13:802.
32 'The first thing', letter to Martha J. Loane 8–10 September 1895, 13:833.
33 'But maternity nursing', 13:834.

Notes to Chapter 5: Workhouse Infirmaries and Hospitals

1 Epigraphs, 6:237 and 248. Much material on the establishment of work-house infirmary nursing is in Chapter 6, *Public Health Care*, of the *Collected Works*.

2 The five to one proportion, from 1861, is quoted from Brian Abel-Smith, *The Hospitals 1800-1948: A Study in Social Administration in England and Wales* (London: Heinemann 1964) 46.

3 Figure 5.1, Letter on workhouse nursing, 6:233-4.

4 'What the broth' 6:397.

5 Figure 5.2, ABCs of workhouse reform, 6:346-7.

6 'Sick, infirm' 6:348.

7 Figure 5.3, letter to Gathorne Hardy, 13:591-2.

8 'Perhaps I', from 'Suggestions on the subject of providing training and organizing nurses,' 6:370.

9 Quotation from Abel-Smith, *The Hospitals*, 82.

10 Epigraph, *Notes on Hospitals*, 1863, 107, vol. 16.

11 'It may seem', Preface, *Notes on Hospitals*, 1863, iii, vol. 16.

12 'If anything', Chapter 1, *Notes on Hospitals*, 1863, 11-12, vol. 16.

13 'If overcrowding', *Notes on Hospitals*, 1863, 13, vol. 16.

14 'proportion of' in Chapter 3, 'Principles of hospital construction', 1863, vol. 16.

15 'The essential feature', Chapter 3, 'Principles of hospital construction', 1863, 56, vol. 16.

16 'As for doctors', letter to Sidney Herbert, 1859, 12:123.

17 'Nursing the sick', in 'Hospitals', *Chambers's Encyclopaedia: A Dictionary of Universal Knowledge* (Edinburgh: W. & R. Chambers 1890), vol. 16.

Notes to Chapter 6: India and Empire

1 Epigraph from 'Observations by Miss Nightingale on the evidence contained in the stational returns', *Report of the Royal Commission on the Sanitary State of the Army in India*, 1863, in 9:136. Two volumes in the *Collected Works* report Indian material, Gerard Vallee, ed., *Health in India*, vol. 9, and *Social Change in India*, vol. 10.

2 'Parable' clipping in 9:44.

3 Figure 6.1, letter 5:425-6.

4 Epigraph, 'The Zemindar, the sun and the watering pot as affecting life and death in India', 10:403.

5 '29 million', from Mike Davis, *Late Victorian Holocausts: El Nino Famines and the Making of the Third World* (London: Verso 2001) 7.

6 'no famine', quotation from Amartya K. Sen, *Development as Freedom* (Oxford: Oxford University Press 1999) 152.

7 Quotations from Mary Scharlieb, *Reminiscences* (London: Williams & Norgate 1924), 10:723.

8 Figure 6.2, Letter to Lady Dufferin, 10:733-4.

9 'Sanitary statistics of native colonial schools and hospitals', 6:168-83.

Recommended Sources on Florence Nightingale

Abel-Smith, Brian. *A History of the Nursing Profession.* London: Heinemann, 1960.
—— *The Hospitals 1800–1948: A Study in Social Administration in England and Wales.* London: Heinemann, 1964.
Baly, Monica E. *Florence Nightingale and the Nursing Legacy.* London: Heinemann, 1973.
Bishop, W. J. and Sue Goldie, (comps.) *A Bio-Bibliography of Florence Nightingale.* London: Dawson, 1962.
Bostridge, Mark. *Florence Nightingale: The Making of a Legend.* London: Farrer, Straus, Giroux 2008, and London: Viking, 2008.
Calabria, Michael D. (ed.) *Florence Nightingale in Egypt and Greece: Her Diary and 'Visions'.* Albany: State University of New York Press, 1987.
Cartwright, Frederick F. *Nightingales and Eagles: The Reform of British Nursing.* Guelph, ON: Typescript, 2001.
Cook, Edward T. *The Life of Florence Nightingale.* 2 vols. London: Macmillan, 1913.
Dossey, Barbara M. *Florence Nightingale: Mystic, Visionary and Healer.* Philadelphia: Springhouse, 1999.
Goldie, Sue. *A Calendar of the Letters of Florence Nightingale.* Oxford: Microform, 1983.
—— (ed.) *'I have Done my Duty': Florence Nightingale in the Crimean War 1854–1856.* Manchester: Manchester University Press, 1987.
Gourlay, Jharna. *Florence Nightingale and the Health of the Raj.* Aldershot Hants: Ashgate, 2003.

Hardy, Gwen. *William Rathbone and the Early History of District Nursing*. Osmskirk: G. W. & A. Hesketh, 1981.

Helmstadter, Carol. 'Florence Nightingale's opposition to state registration of nurses'. *Nursing History Review* 15 (2007):155–66.

Herbert, Raymond G. (ed.) *Florence Nightingale: Saint, Reformer or Rebel?* Malabar, FL: Krieger, 1981.

Hutchison, John F. *Champions of Charity: War and the Rise of the Red Cross*. Boulder: Westview, 1996.

Luddy, Maria (ed.) *The Crimean Journals of the Sisters of Mercy 1854–56*. Dublin: Four Courts, 2004.

McDonald, Lynn, 'Florence Nightingale', in Lynn McDonald (ed.) *The Women Founders of the Social Sciences*. Montreal QC: McGill Queen's University Press 1994: 183–211.

—— ed., 'Florence Nightingale (1820–1910)', in *Women Theorists on Society and Politics*. Waterloo ON: Wilfrid Laurier University Press 1998: 165–202.

——'Florence Nightingale: passionate statistician'. *Journal of Holistic Nursing* 16, 2 (June 1998): 267–77.

—— 'Florence Nightingale and the early origins of evidence-based nursing'. *Evidence-Based Nursing* 4, 3 (July 2001): 68–9.

—— ed. *Collected Works of Florence Nightingale*. 16 vols. Waterloo: Wilfrid Laurier University Press, 2001.

——'Florence Nightingale as a social reformer'. *History Today* 56, 1 (January 2006): 9–15.

—— 'Florence Nightingale and European wars: from the Crimean to the Franco-Prussian War'. *Leidschrift* 22, 2 (September 2007): 145–60.

Nutting, M. Adelaide and Lavinia L. Dock. *A History of Nursing: The Evolution of Nursing Systems from the Earliest Times to the Foundation of the First English and American Training Schools for Nurses*. 4 vols. Bristol: Thoemmes Press reprint, 1997–2002.

O'Malley, I. B. *Florence Nightingale 1820–56: A Study of Her Life Down to the End of the Crimean War*. London: Butterworth, 1931.

Seymer, Lucy Ridgely. *Florence Nightingale's Nurses: The Nightingale Training School 1860–1960*. London: Pitman Medical, 1960.

Shepherd, John. *The Crimean Doctors: A History of the British Medical Services in the Crimean War*. 2 vols. Liverpool: Liverpool University Press, 1991.

Skretkowicz, Victor (ed.) *Notes on Nursing*. London: Baillière Tindall, 1996.

Stone, Richard. 'Florence Nightingale and hospital reform', in Richard Stone (ed.) *Some British Empiricists in the Social Sciences 1650–1900*. Cambridge: Cambridge University Press/Raffaele Mattioli Foundation 1997: 303–37.

Sullivan, Mary C. *The Friendship of Florence Nightingale and Mary Clare Moore*. Philadelphia: University of Pennsylvania Press, 1999.

Vicinus, Martha and Bea Nergaard (eds) *Ever Yours, Florence Nightingale: Selected Letters*. Cambridge MA: Harvard University Press, 1990.

Whiteside, Carol Lea. *The Sources and Forms of Power used by Florence Nightingale as Depicted in her Letters Written July 1, 1853 to August 7, 1856*. Gonzaga University doctoral thesis, 2004.

Index

Abbott, Jacob 8, 54, 58
Aberdeen, Lady 124
Aberdeen, Lord 124
Afghanistan 166, 179
Alexander, Thomas 76, 161
Anglican 23, 52, 57, 71, 132 (*see also*
  Church of England)
Anglo-Zulu War 91
antiseptic/aseptic 101–4, 111–13, 127
Antoninus, Marcus Aurelius 46

Balaclava 70, 152–3
Barrack Hospital 2, 67, 71–2, 75, 79,
  83–5, 90, 143, 152–3
Belfast 13, 114–18, 150
Bellevue Hospital 113, 122–3
Bence Jones, Henry 142
Bismarck, Chancellor 93
Blackwell, Elizabeth 49
Boer War 91
Bonham Carter, Hilary 48–9
Bonham Carter, Henry xvii, 25, 104,
  109–12
Bracebridge, Charles H. 6
Bracebridge, Selina xvii, 6, 24, 44, 48
Bunsen, Christian von 76

Calvin, John 54–5
Campbell, George 166

Canada/Canadian 49, 76, 89, 114,
  122–4, 172–3, 178
Cassandra 53–4, 60–4, 179
Cavour, Count Camillo Benso di
  44–5
Chadwick, Edwin 48, 145–7
childbirth 35, 130, 132, 135, 138 (*see
  also* maternity, midwifery)
children's hospitals/wards 114,
  156–7
cholera 70, 78, 81, 101–3, 111, 161
Christ 11, 58–9, 61, 65, 111 (*see also*
  Jesus)
Christian/ity 7–9, 16, 46, 55, 58–9, 97,
  110–11, 143, 171, 178
Church of England 3, 8–9, 52 (*see also*
  Anglican)
Churchill, Randolph 37
Civil War (American) 89–91
Clark, James 75
Comte, Auguste 28, 52, 55
Conservative (Party) 51, 144, 14–8
Contagious Diseases Acts 17, 51, 179
  (*see also* prostitute)
Creator 8, 30, 44 (*see also* God)
Crimean War 2, 6, 16, 19–20, 32, 41,
  48, 67–90, 94–5, 99, 101, 142, 151–2,
  161–2, 172 (see also Barrack)
Croft, John 102

Dante 41

Darwin, Charles 30

Darwinism 31

death/death rate 2, 10, 22–3, 28, 70–4, 84, 87, 91, 112, 130–8, 144, 151–2, 154, 159–60, 168, 173, 178 (*see also* mortality)

disinfectant 102–4, 112–13, 127, 131, 139

Disraeli, Benjamin 37

Dublin 114–5

Dufferin, Lady xvii, 50, 170–2

Egypt (campaign, war in) 18, 21, 48, 91, 121, 124
   Nightingale in 1, 6–7, 27, 38

Ekblom, Ellen 105, 112

Eugenie, Empress 40

evangelical 8, 54, 143, 179

Farr, William xvii, 29, 48, 74, 78, 102, 154, 161, 177

Fliedner, Caroline 7

Fliedner, Theodor 7, 95

France/French
   Nightingale in 1, 5, 38–40
   other, general 1, 9, 38–41, 68–70, 89, 132, 155–6

Franco-Prussian War 14, 18, 48–9, 91–6

Galton, Francis 36

Garibaldi, Giuseppe de 45–7

Garrett Anderson, Elizabeth 50

Geneva Convention 91–2

German/y 1, 5, 9, 27, 29, 39, 94–6, 102, 175

germs/germ theory 101–3, 113, 155

Girton College, Cambridge 48–9

Gladstone, W.E. 95–6

God 7–11, 15, 19, 21–2, 27–32, 37, 41, 44, 46, 48, 51–9, 63–5, 99, 110, 143, 178–9

government (general) 17, 27–9, 31–47, 65, 77–8, 80, 92, 143–5, 159, 162–8, 173, 177

Guido Reni 43

Hall, John 2, 73, 76, 84–5

Hardy, Gathorne xvii, 144, 147–9

Helena, grand duchess 70

Herbert, Elizabeth 44, 70

Herbert, Sidney xvii, 13–14, 23, 45, 70, 76, 85, 150, 156, 161

Herbert Hospital 23, 156

Hill, Octavia 49

hospitals (general, other) 2, 6, 13–14, 20, 25, 29, 33–4, 49, 61, 67, 78, 85, 91, 99–100, 104, 106–8, 110–27, 130–6, 138, 141–58, 161, 167, 170, 172–3, 175–8 (*see also* Barrack, children's, Herbert, King's College, lying-in, maternity, military, St Bartholomew's, St Thomas')

Ignatius of Loyola 54, 57–8

Ilbert Bill 164–5

India/n 2–3, 7, 11, 17–19, 25–6, 31, 34, 50, 103, 159–73, 177–9
   famine in 14, 36, 160, 160, 163, 166–8, 177, 179

Irby, Adeline Paulina 49

Italy/ian 1, 5, 6, 16, 38–41, 44–6, 52, 54, 56, 92, 118, 131

Jesus 3, 12, 52, 97 (*see also* Christ)
Johns Hopkins University Hospital 123–4
Jones, Agnes E. xvii, 143–4, 150
Jones, Mary 23, 132
Jowett, Benjamin xvii, 10–11, 23, 129
Julius Caesar 40

Kaiserswerth Deaconess Institution 1, 7, 15, 23, 95
King's College Hospital 74, 130–2, 155
Koch, Robert 102–3

Lawrence, John 163
laws (of nature) 9, 27–30, 35, 64, 179
Lees, Florence 122, 137
Le Fort, Leon 131–3
Liberal Party 2–3, 37, 144, 147, 169
Longmore, Thomas 92
Louis-Napoleon (Napoleon III) 39–40, 44, 93
Louis-Philippe 39–40
lying-in hospital 114, 129, 131–5 (*see also* maternity)

Machin, Maria 124
marriage 11, 53, 59, 61–2, 65
    child marriage 168–9
Martineau, Harriet xvii, 5, 48, 51, 54, 69, 78, 91
maternity (hospital/ward) 129–36, 138, 141, 155 (*see also* lying-in, midwifery)
Mazzini, Giuseppe 45–6
Macleod, Charlotte 124
McNeill, John xvii, 74–5

medical school/science 47, 77, 101, 117, 129
Michelangelo 15
midwifery nursing 49, 74, 129–39 (*see also* lying-in, maternity)
militarism 67, 91–7
military hospital 86, 153, 155–6, 162–3
Mill, John Stuart xvii, 9, 21, 52, 147, 149, 179
Milnes, Richard Monckton 10
Mohl, Mary Clarke 48
mortality 10, 72, 78, 82, 85, 87, 89, 91, 129–36, 152–4, 156, 173, 177 (*see also* death)
Muslim 7, 69, 170

Naoroji, Dadabhai 160
Napoleon Bonaparte 38, 40, 42–3, 80
Napoleon III (*see* Louis-Napoleon)
Napoleonic Wars 69
Newcastle, Duke of 86, 172
Newnham College, Cambridge 48
Newton, Isaac 27, 30
Nightingale, Frances xvii, 6, 17, 60, 114
Nightingale Fund/Trust 10, 12, 15, 25, 34, 74, 109, 130
Nightingale, Parthenope (Lady Verney) xvii, 2, 6–7, 9, 11, 17, 20, 22
Nightingale, W.E. xvii, xv, 1, 5, 8, 10, 12, 30, 32, 45, 60, 115
nursing 1, 3, 6, 8, 10, 12–19, 22–3, 33, 35, 44, 47–50, 54–5, 57, 67, 69–74, 76, 89, 93, 99–139, 141–51, 154, 156–8, 160, 162–3, 167, 169, 173, 175–9 (*see also* midwifery)

Oxford 30, 36, 111

Panmure, Lord xvii, 74–6
Paris 1, 14, 38–40, 60, 73, 93, 96, 119, 133, 135, 146, 155–6
Pius IX 6, 41–4
Poor Law 17, 34, 37, 48, 96, 101, 141, 144, 148, 150, 176 (*see also* workhouse)
positivim/t 28–9, 52
Pringle, Angelique Lucille xvii, 111, 124
prostitute/ion 47, 50–1, 96, 162, 179 (*see also* Contagious Diseases)
Protestant 9, 43, 54, 56–9, 106, 114, 175
Prussia (*see* Franco-Prussian)
Prussia, crown princess of 93
puerperal fever 130, 132–4, 138

Quain, Richard 125
Quain's *Dictionary of Medicine* 103, 113, 125–7
Quetelet, L.A.J. 9, 27–8, 35–6, 177

Raglan, Lord 73, 79–85
Rathbone, William xvii, 13, 18, 33, 122, 136, 143, 149
Rawlinson, Robert 32, 48, 74
Red Cross 91–3
Richards, Linda 123
Robb, Isabel Hampton 123
Roman Catholic 1, 9, 21, 52, 54, 56–60, 106, 111, 115
Rome 1, 6–7, 15, 38, 41–8, 57, 70, 114

St Bartholomew's Hospital 107, 121, 153, 156
St Thomas' Hospital 14, 18–20, 24–5, 74, 103–4, 108, 110–16, 122–4, 151, 153, 158
sanitary condition/reform/science 8, 19, 32, 48, 72, 75, 77–78, 80, 82, 83, 87–9, 101, 112, 116, 124, 137, 146, 151, 153, 159, 161–3, 170–2
Savonarola 41
Scharlieb, Mary 50, 168–70
science 24, 27–31, 36, 52, 59, 65, 77, 114, 117, 129 (*see also* medical, social)
Scutari 2, 6, 16, 70–4, 79–81, 83–90, 95, 143, 152–4 (*see also* Barrack Hospital)
Semmelweiss, Ignacz 131–2
Senior, Jane 48–9
Shaftesbury, Lord 21, 151
Shelley, Percy Bysshe 16, 54
Simpson, James Y. 132
Smith, Andrew 76, 83, 85–6
Smith, Mary Shore xvii, 22, 55, 73–4, 79
Smith, Robert Angus 31, 148
Smith, Rosalind Shore 49
Smith, William 21, 90
Smith, William Shore 22
social science 19, 27–30, 96, 151, 177
Stanley, Lord 160–1
Suggestions for Thought 11, 24, 27, 31, 51–65, 179
Sutherland, John xvii, 13, 35, 48, 74, 102–3, 144, 161
syphilis 50, 162, 179

Teresa, St 59
Trevelyan, Charles 161–2
typhus 73, 101, 144

Unitarian Church 8, 54, 58
United States 90, 97, 122–4, 175, 178
    (*see also* America)

Verney, Harry xvii, 2, 11, 14, 17, 21,
    25, 37, 41, 45, 47, 110
Victoria, Queen 18, 50, 75, 93, 124,
    132, 137, 159, 164–5, 170

Vienna 50, 103, 118–22, 131
Villiers, C.P. xvii, 144, 148

Wardroper, Sarah E. xvii, 108–9
Wesleyan 9, 23
Westminster, Duke of 12
Wilhelm II 96
Worcester, Alfred 124
workhouse infirmaries 13, 18, 25,
    33, 35–6, 53, 114, 133, 135, 138,
    141–51, 175–7 (*see also* Poor
    Law)

Made in the USA
Middletown, DE
13 February 2018